praise for
APRICOTS ON THE NILE

"Reading this [book] is like spending an afternoon in the kitchen with a beloved older relative. What could be better than hearing tales of an exotic past while preparing the foods that are at the core of the shared memories? [A] tasty treat for both body and soul."

—*Publishers Weekly*

"If you like to know the cook behind the cookbook, Colette Rossant delivers in both areas. Seekers of a good story won't be disappointed either. . . . [E]vocative . . . a fascinating journey."

—Epicurious.com

Also by Colette Rossant

Return to Paris

APRICOTS ON THE NILE

A Memoir with Recipes

Colette Rossant

WASHINGTON SQUARE PRESS
NEW YORK   LONDON   TORONTO   SYDNEY

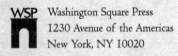

WSP Washington Square Press
1230 Avenue of the Americas
New York, NY 10020

Previously published as *Memories of a Lost Egypt* by Clarkson Potter

ISBN: 0-7434-7561-5

First Washington Square Press trade paperback edition April 2004

10 9 8 7 6 5 4 3 2 1

WASHINGTON SQUARE PRESS and colophon are
registered trademarks of Simon & Schuster, Inc.

Manufactured in the United States of America

For information regarding special discounts for bulk purchases, please contact
Simon & Schuster Special Sales at 1-800-456-6798 or
business@simonandschuster.com

TO MY GRANDCHILDREN

Matthew, Julien, and Celine, Luca, and Oliver

AND TO THOSE NOT YET BORN.

I WANT TO THANK MY CHILDREN,
who for many years listened to my stories
and urged me to write them down. A special
thanks goes to my oldest daughter, Marianne,
who carefully read every chapter, asking
questions and making valuable suggestions.
A heartfelt thanks goes to my agent and
friend, Gloria Loomis, who encouraged
me to write this book; to my editor,
Roy Finamore, who trusted me and did a
beautiful job of editing; and to my husband
and friend, James, who has stood by me all
these years.

Contents

LIST OF RECIPES

LIST OF ILLUSTRATIONS

CHAPTER I
My Mother

I AM PEELING SHRIMP FOR MY MOTHER. MOST LIKELY, she'll refuse them. She eats nothing at the Mother Cabrini Hospice, where she is dying of cancer. Three months ago, the doctors gave her three months to live; it is clear to me that she has no intention of dying yet, as if hanging on were a matter of spiteful retaliation. She complains all the time in a whiny French voice, especially when attendants are hovering near her bed. Each time the dietitian asks her what she'd like, my mother answers, "Chinese shrimp with vegetables," as if she's in Chinatown. I have finally found the time to prepare this fantasy dish in my own kitchen, convinced that the greasy version from a restaurant will kill her. Perhaps I should have gone for the take-out.

I visit her every afternoon. When I come in, she is usually asleep, or at least pretends to be. The television is always on, with the sound turned off. She lies still, her face turned toward the television, her eyes closed. The skin of her face is very taut. Her head looks like a skull with an immense forehead because her hair is pushed all the way up. I sit on a dark brown leatherette chair and wait for her to wake up. Her hands, with their perfectly manicured nails, lie still beside her thighs. She was always proud of her long-fingered, elegant hands. Mine show the signs of washing, cooking, and gardening: short, jagged nails; swollen knuckles; heavy cuticle moons. I used to be very jealous of her hands, but I've since found revenge through my three daughters, who have magnificent hands. The Haitian nurse comes in to look at her, checks her breathing, and leaves. When my mother is awake, she tells me—in French—how vulgar she finds the nurse's nails, which are very long and airbrushed with intricate designs and sprays of glitter. Once a week I bring the nurse chocolate to appease my guilt, and to make sure my mother doesn't receive retaliation in the guise of care.

My mother wakes up and looks at me. She is silent and unsmiling.

"I brought you some Chinese shrimp. You want to try some?" I say. She continues to stare at me in silence.

"What time is it?" she asks suddenly, minutes later.

"Half past five. Do you want to try to eat? The shrimps? They're still hot." With irritation etched on her mouth, she rasps, "I'm not hungry. I'll eat later."

There are long silences between us. We never talk about anything that is important: God, love, my father, her life without us, how she met my stepfather—who had died a few years earlier—or why she became Catholic when she had been raised in the Jewish faith. My father died in Aswan when I was six. I vaguely remember him.

My mother never talks about him, and I always avoid bringing this subject up as I know from experience that our conversation will lead nowhere. I don't know why. When he died, she left me for four years with my Egyptian grandparents. I never knew what she really felt about me, and I still don't know today. When we went back to Paris after the war, she again left me, this time with her mother, and I did not see her until I was twenty. When I moved to the United States with my husband, she wanted to follow us to New York. I think she was lonely and she thought that we would be friends and that I would let her come into my life. It never happened. I made sure that she lived nearby but never with us. We always pretended that we loved each other, but I had built myself a world of memories where my mother is nowhere to be found. I want it to stay that way.

It is six—time for Father Paul's visit. He comes in, smiling. "How is my girl today?" My mother beams, slightly flirty, and tells him she's just fine. Maybe now she'll eat. As the priest leaves, I plead, "You want to taste the shrimp? They'll get cold if you don't eat them now." She tries one, then another, and finally smiles like a small child who has gotten what she wants. "They're good but they're not Chinese," she says petulantly as she pushed the plate away and closes her eyes. She dozes off and I wait, flipping through the thick photo album by her bed. There are many pictures—in tones of pale gray—of my mother when she was young. She is at the beach . . . in a convertible . . . at her wedding. I gaze at her lush, tall body in a long, white satin dress with the undulating waves of a train arranged behind her and a heavy, cascading bouquet in her hand. My father is taller than she and darkly handsome like an Arab prince. There are pictures of them on their honeymoon in Venice, then in Paris on their balcony. Then page after page of my brother, and just a few of me. There is a picture of me in Cairo in my grandparents' house. My brother and I are sitting on a white Victorian couch with a gilded frame. I am an adorable little girl with curly hair and a shy smile. I look at these pictures with a smile; I feel very tender toward that little girl.

I am painfully pulled from the beginning of a journey I was afraid to take by my mother's strangely low voice. "I was beautiful," she says, as if she had never fallen asleep. She had been, in all her heavy curves and thick auburn hair, and large, lazy hands. Whenever she would take me in her arms and pressed my little child's body against her, I'd flash back to one of the only times she took me food shopping, a job normally undertaken by my governess or the cook. I was four at the time, and while my mother was ordering something, my curious eyes spotted an enormous hill of sweet butter. I suddenly felt the urge to bury my hands in it. It looked and smelled so good, I went for it. The saleswoman screamed, my mother slapped me, and my hands were retrieved from the yellow hill. I tried to lick them, but my buttered hands were pulled out of my mouth. My mother wiped my hands, apologized, paid for the damages, and dragged me out of the store. She never took me shopping again with her, and from that day, whenever she drew me close to her, I thought of her as a large lump of butter, except her smell was not as pleasant. She used a heavy carnation-scented perfume that turned my stomach. I would push her away, saying, "You smell terrible." "Well, you stink of garlic!" my mother would answer. And it was true, since I liked dunking a piece of fresh baguette into a dish of crushed garlic marinating in olive oil and seasoned with salt and pepper that Georgette, my grandmother's cook, often prepared for me, instead of the traditional *petit pain au chocolat* that most French children ate with relish.

AS WE ENTER her room, Thomas's voice booms, "Hi Grandma, look what I brought you. *Semits,* the ones you like— have a piece." My mother looks up and smiles, greeting him warmly. She tries a small piece of the pretzel, chews, and tries hard to swallow. "Don't force her," I say, "and give her something to drink." They both ignore me. He saunters around her bed, chatting away, telling her about his girlfriend, whom he wants to marry. "Get better quickly . . . you must come to the wedding."

I am back in the armchair, looking at the album. There is a picture of me taken in Paris—wrapped up in a large shawl; large eyes, accentuated by thick black lashes, peering out of the intricately colored material. I must have been about four when we lived in a large Paris apartment near the Parc Monceau. My father was the European buyer for his father's large department store in Cairo. A Swiss governess, Marie-Louise, took care of my brother and me. By the time I was two, my father had become ill and my mother decided that I should spend some time at her parents' apartment on the avenue de la Grande Armée, near the Étoile. My father needed

SEMIT

Semits are soft pretzels with a crispy crust covered with sesame seeds. They are piled high in baskets and sold in the streets of Cairo.

HEAT 1¼ CUPS MILK in a saucepan, but do not boil it. Add ¾ cup water, 2 tablespoons each lard and butter, 2½ tablespoons sugar, and 1 tablespoon salt. Mix well and cool until the mixture is tepid.

DISSOLVE ¾ OUNCE DRIED YEAST in ½ cup water with a pinch of sugar. Wait until the yeast is frothy, then pour it into a bowl with the milk mixture. Add 7 cups of flour, mixing gently with a wooden spoon until you have a soft dough that detaches itself from the sides of the bowl. Form into a ball, wrap in foil, and allow to rest for 10 minutes.

KNEAD THE DOUGH on a floured board until smooth and elastic, about 15 minutes. Divide the dough into 4 pieces. Shape each piece into a ring about 4 inches in diameter and ¾ inch thick. Dip into an egg beaten with 2 tablespoons water, then dip into a bowl filled with 2 cups sesame seeds.

OIL A BAKING SHEET. Place the rings on the sheet, cover lightly, and set aside in a warm, draft-free place until they double in size.

BAKE IN A PREHEATED 450-degree oven for 10 minutes. Reduce the heat to 350 degrees and bake for 20 minutes, or until golden brown.

a lot of care and quiet, and my mother used to tell her parents that I was very noisy. I did not really care because I liked their apartment with its long corridor leading from the entrance hall to the kitchen. This is where I learned to roller-skate. And then there was Georgette, the old-maid cook who ruled the kitchen, which was always open to me. I can see her slim body bent over a heavy saucepan, a wooden spoon in her hand, tasting a sauce, peeling potatoes or chopping shallots for the evening meal. I would rollerskate to the kitchen, perch on a high stool, and watch her cook. Inevitably, my grandmother would catch on and oblige me to leave the kitchen. *"Une jeune fille de bonne famille ne fréquente pas la cuisine!"* ("A young girl of good breeding does not go into the kitchen!") I'd try the living room after that, gazing out the French windows overlooking the avenue. It was furnished with a Louis XVI petit point couch and armchairs, wonderful stained-glass lamps on inlaid tables, and a very ornate crystal chandelier. In one corner of the room was a grand piano. I used to hide under it. It was covered with a very large embroidered Egyptian shawl, maybe a present from my Egyptian grandparents. Sometimes I would wrap it around myself, cover half my face, and proclaim that I was the Queen of Egypt. My grandmother would be very upset. "Get out of there," she would cry. "You are not Egyptian, you are French!" Looking again at that photograph of me made on our first trip to Cairo when I was barely four, I think I did look Egyptian.

Sometimes Georgette would take me to the market with her. She would stop in a front of a stand piled with fresh herbs—thyme, marjoram, tarragon. She'd squeeze a leaf or two between her fingers and sniff. "Mmm . . . these are very fragrant. Smell, Colette." And I would smell and approve her choice. My favorite day was mussels day. The whole house smelled of garlic and parsley cooking in butter. I'd wait in the kitchen for lunch to be ready, but my grandmother would get angry with us. *"Tu sens la cuisine! Va-t'en!"* ("You smell like the kitchen! Get out of here!"), she would say in disgust.

I preferred Grandpère James to my grandmother. He was shorter than his wife, with a round belly. He wore pince-nez, which made him look like a stern teacher, though he was not.

MUSSELS MARINIÈRE

MELT 2 TABLESPOONS BUTTER in a large saucepan. Add 1/2 cup chopped parsley and 3 minced garlic cloves and sauté for 3 minutes. Add salt and pepper to taste, then 4 pints of mussels (bearded and well scrubbed) and 1 cup white wine. Cover and cook over medium heat, shaking the pan several times, for 10 minutes, or until the mussels have opened.

DIVIDE THE MUSSELS among 4 soup plates. Strain the liquid and pour over the mussels. Serve with a French baguette.

My grandfather loved everything English. I was told, years later, that at the age of eighteen he had changed his first name to James and his last name to Bémant. I never did find out what his real name was. I always knew when he was upset: he would remove his pince-nez several times and clean it with his handkerchief. He was a dental surgeon who had made his fortune as an inventor of special steel for dental surgery. Every Saturday he took me for walks in the park; then we would end up in a *salon de thé* for pastries and hot chocolate. My grand-father loved food. He had put on weight, and the *salon de thé* was our secret, to be kept from my grandmother. I disliked pastries but never let on, as I did not want to disappoint him. I would order his favorite cake, take a bite, say I wasn't hungry, and my grandfather would finish his cake and mine. We would walk back home, hand in hand, pleased with ourselves for having fooled my grandmother.

Grandmother Rose was the opposite. She was tall—like my mother—with a large bosom and a very thin waist. She was corseted from chin to thighs. I liked to lie on her bed while she dressed, fascinated by her corset with its hundreds of grommeted holes where the laces went through. While dressing, she'd advise me as if I were about to become a bride: "Never undress in front of your husband; keep the mystery." Or, "Always look pretty, even in the kitchen." Although I didn't understand these words of wisdom, I listened attentively since it was the only time she paid attention to me. Sometimes she would take me to the park with my brother. She always wore a large hat decorated with flowers or birds about to fly away; a *voilette* would hide her face. Sometimes men would follow her in the street, murmuring words I did not understand, but I knew they pleased her. I would try to see what or who had made her smile, but her steps would quicken and she would say, "Let's hurry, we are late for tea; and don't look back!"

There is a knock at the door, and the nurse comes in with a tray. "Dinner," she says cheerfully. I look up at my mother. There is a sly expression on her face; I am afraid she is going to say something nasty to the young nurse, but my son is quick to take over. "Let's eat something. Do you want to start with the soup?" He feeds her a spoon or two; she eats to please him. I can see she is very tired; her eyes are now closed. My son looks worried and tries to talk to her but she does not answer. Thomas is upset. He bends toward her and says, "We're going, Grandma. I'll see you next week." She smiles wearily and turns her head toward Thomas for a kiss. As I wait for him in the car, I see myself at age five, leaving again for Egypt, saying goodbye to my grandfather James and feeling lost at the idea of leaving him behind. That summer, my brother and I accompanied my French grandparents to Biarritz, where they owned a house surrounded by a large garden. My father had to be operated on in Geneva, and we were to join my parents later in the south of France.

Georgette loved Biarritz, the Atlantic coast resort town, where she could prepare all her favorite dishes because my grandparents had lots of guests on weekends. We all ate in the garden on long wooden table. The lunches would drag on for hours, and I had to wait for Grandmother Rose to nod toward me; only then could I leave the table and run to the kitchen and Georgette. This was the only summer I remember when my grandmother allowed me in the kitchen. I would sit on a stool and watch Georgette prepare a tomato salad. She would place ripe red tomatoes in a bowl of boiling water, leave them there for a few minutes, then refresh them under cold water and show me how easily the skin slipped away. Sometimes I helped; I would be given the task of preparing the herbs, cutting the leaves away from the stems of tarragon, sage, or parsley. My favorite was chervil, which Georgette used in her lettuce salad. But the best time I had in the kitchen was when Georgette made chicken soup. We would go to the butcher

TOMATO SALAD

BRING A POT OF WATER to a boil. Turn off the heat and add 5 large ripe tomatoes. Take them out after 3 minutes and cool under cold running water. Slip off the skins.

IN A LARGE BOWL, mix together 2 shallots and 1 clove of garlic—both peeled and minced—with 2 tablespoons olive oil and 1 tablespoon lemon juice. Add salt and pepper to taste. Slice the tomatoes and add them to the bowl. Toss well, sprinkle with 1 tablespoon minced fresh tarragon or fresh chervil, and serve at room temperature. This will serve 4 to 6.

together, and she would ask the butcher for some marrowbones. *"Pour la petite,"* she would say, pointing at me. Then later, when the soup was done, she would remove one marrowbone from the soup and with a tiny spoon place the marrow on a piece of baguette, sprinkle it with salt, and give it to me. The warm, slightly gelatinous marrow would slide down my throat, its strong meaty taste filling my mouth. The other marrowbones would be served at dinner with onion *confit.* If Grandmother Rose caught us, we were in trouble. "You are making her fat! It is not good for children!"

The news came that my father had had a stroke. He was now paralyzed and blind. We all drove back to Paris. At the time I didn't understand what being paralyzed was, and my brother, two years older than I, explained that my father could not move, not even walk. Everyone had to take care of him,

MARROWBONES WITH ONION CONFIT

WASH 6 BEEF MARROWBONES under cold running water. Heat 8 cups of chicken broth in a large saucepan. Stick an onion with 2 cloves and cut a carrot and a stalk of celery into 1-inch pieces and add to the broth. Simmer for 15 minutes. Add the marrowbones and simmer for 20 minutes. Then remove the bones to a baking pan with a slotted spoon and bake in a preheated 400-degree oven until golden brown, about 15 minutes.

PLACE EACH MARROWBONE on a plate with a teaspoon of coarse salt near it. Garnish with onion *confit.*

TO MAKE THE *CONFIT*, peel and thinly slice 6 large Vidalia onions. Melt 3 tablespoons butter in a large saucepan, add the onions, and cook, stirring with a wooden spoon over medium heat, until the onions are golden brown. Add ½ cup red wine and salt and pepper to taste, lower the heat, and simmer, covered, for 40 minutes, stirring from time to time. If the onions start to stick to the bottom, stir in ¼ cup of the marrowbone broth. This dish will serve 6.

and I had to be very quiet and nice. Several weeks later, summoned by my Egyptian grandfather, the entire family, along with a male nurse and our governess, left for Egypt.

Thomas joins me in the car; he looks unhappy and worried. "She looks bad. . . . I won't be able to come back until next Thursday. Do you think it's okay?" I don't answer since I am still in my memory's hold, saying goodbye to my grandfather

James. It must have been 1937. He hugged me and whispered that we would see each other the following summer. I kept on saying to him, "I'll see you next week," but he simply embraced me. I never saw him again. War was declared two years later, and he died before my mother brought me back to Paris. Thomas interrupts my reverie. "She's dying," he says sadly. We drive in silence; tomorrow I have to speak to the doctor.

I AM LATE for the visit. The Haitian nurse takes me aside and whispers that my mother won't last long, is there anything she can do? I shake my head and go into the room. My mother's eyes are closed; she is not really conscious of my presence. I sit in my usual place and wait. Her hands are outside the covers, still, on the white sheet. There are large blotches of purple, bruises from the I.V. I don't understand how they are able to stick a needle in her hand—her skin is transparent as parchment. I take her hand and squeeze it; there is no response. Today I don't want to stay. I leave, telling the nurse I will be back early tomorrow. At eleven that night, the telephone rings. It's my mother's nurse. My mother died half an hour ago.

I return to the hospice with Marianne, my oldest daughter. I sit once more in the armchair and look at my mother. She looks very peaceful, her eyes closed, her mouth in a faint smile. I look around the room. There are very few personal things: her toiletry bag, her missal, the photo album. I feel relieved I won't have to come back. I tell the nurse that the funeral home will take care of everything. My mother wanted to be cremated, with her ashes thrown into the sea. I don't know how or where to do this, but I will find a way. Once this last deed is done, I can feel free.

CHAPTER 2

The House

MY GOVERNESS MARIE-LOUISE, WHOM I CALLED MALOU, had just finished smoothing out the ringlets on my five-year-old head as we docked at Alexandria in the spring of 1937. Malou, dressed in her navy blue uniform, her own hair tucked beneath a blue-and-white nurse's veil, clutched my hand tightly as we descended the gangplank. She pointed to a tall man with white hair, waving frantically from the dock below. "It's your grandfather Vita," she said. "Wave back!" I was jumping up and down, wanting to run to him, but

Malou admonished me in a stern voice. When we were halfway down, I heard a voice shouting, *"Semit!... Semit!... Semit!"* It came from a young boy in a dirty gray robe with a large basket filled with pretzels perched on his head and hiding his face. "I want one! I want one!" I cried. Malou shook her head, muttering under her breath, "Never! They're disgusting...too dirty." Suddenly I was picked up, embraced mightily, and handed a *semit* by the white-haired stranger whom Malou had pointed out to me minutes earlier. I had been right to insist on trying one: the semit was hot, sweet, and crusty like a fresh baguette, and covered with toasted sesame seeds that crackled under my teeth. My grandfather laughed at my delight and, taking me by the hand, led me toward the exit, followed by a frowning Malou. After a four-hour trip through the desert, we arrived in Cairo.

Malou was unhappy. The Cairo heat made her miserable, and she disliked the food, complaining that it was too oily, that nothing was really clean, and that there was no discipline in the household. She was quite upset because my grandmother Marguerite was taking care of me while my mother and father were settling down. Four weeks after our arrival, Malou announced that she was going back to Switzerland and left Egypt without regrets.

My grandparents lived in Garden City, a residential neighborhood with winding streets lined with immense villas surrounded by lush gardens, a neighborhood designed for the nineteenth-century well-to-do Egyptian and European Jewish merchants and foreign ambassadors. Our house, built in the 1890s by my great-grandfather, was a block from the Nile. It was solid, square, and made of stone in the French Mediterranean style. The ground-floor wall was rusticated

limestone; the upper floors were fashioned of smooth limestone blocks supporting continuous balconies and interrupted by tall French windows. The ground floor had
windows looking onto a large terrace facing the quiet street.
The front garden was separated from the street by a wrought-
iron fence decorated with a pair of back-to-back brass *P*'s for
the name Palacci, a Sephardic Spanish surname meaning "of
the palace." Mohammed, the guardian, would polish these *P*'s
until they gleamed.

Behind the fence, the shallow front garden was protected
by tall bushes and trees that hid the terrace from passersby.
The thick stone balustrade was too high for me to see over
into the garden. I used to stick my head between the fat balus-
ters until one day my head became wedged. I can remember
my grandfather spanking me very hard. I remember this incident even today because I had been really scared, thinking I
would never be able to remove my head from the stone
balustrade and because I had never been spanked so hard. My
head ached for days afterward. On the terrace was a rattan
couch and several armchairs on which the family would sit at
dusk every day. A jasmine vine grew over the back garden wall,
and its intoxicating fragrance invaded the terrace. Purple and
red bougainvillea grew resplendently in ornate clay pots by the
exterior walls, and a stately mango tree dominated the garden
and gave us welcome shade in late afternoon. On my first day
in Cairo, Grandpère Vita led me to the tree and told me that
he had planted it the day I was born. I believed him then, but
in retrospect I realized that this was one of the stories he often
fabricated to make me feel special.

A narrow path led from the street to the entrance of the
house, which was on the side and could barely be seen from the

street. The unassuming narrow wooden door belied the grandeur of the wide entrance hall lit by wall sconces and the European magnificence of the broad, curving marble staircase. Each floor landing revealed a painting; on the ground floor was a portrait of an exotic oriental princess with heavily kohl-darkened eyes—her red silk dress all bejeweled, her face half covered with a translucent gold cloth attached to her headdress by a ring of gold, and her shoulders draped with a Spanish shawl. My aunt Fortuné, who lived on the second floor, had painted it from an old photograph. The "princess" was my great-great-grandmother, who had left Turkey to follow her handsome husband to Egypt, and her outfit was a costume she had worn to a costume ball. However, as a matter of course she had worn the veil when she went out, following the practice in Istanbul, where even Jewish women covered their faces. My grandfather Vita, like his ancestors before him, had also traveled to Turkey to find his wife. His forefathers had escaped the Spanish Inquisition, moving eventually to Istanbul. In the sixteenth century, one of his ancestors was appointed majordomo of the Ottoman army. When Turkey invaded Egypt, he, his wife, and their ten children ended up staying in Cairo. However, they all kept ties with Istanbul, and the eldest son in every generation had gone back to Turkey to find a wife. It was my father who broke with tradition and went to Europe, seeking an education and a French wife. Ironically, he, too, ended up in Cairo.

My parents and I settled in with my grandparents, who lived on the ground floor; the rest of the house was filled with extended family. Tante Fortuné (my father's older sister), her husband, and their three children were one flight up; on the third floor lived Oncle Albert, my grandfather's brother, with his wife and three children.

I remember the large salon, and photographs in my mother's album help fill in details. Painted a pale green with white trim, the salon was furnished with a white gilded sofa; gilded petit point armchairs that my grandmother had embroidered; small antique tables inlaid with mother of pearl; and a crystal chandelier that, when lit, would throw swathes of shadow and light on the oriental rugs. On one wall was a glassed-in niche where my grandmother kept her collection of Limoges porcelain and other knickknacks collected over the years. Two French windows opened onto the terrace; during the day the shutters would be half closed so that the brilliant sunlight would not fade the upholstery. The dining room was simply furnished with a long mahogany table that could seat fourteen people; a credenza where the "nice dishes" were kept; and near the windows, two very tall Chinese vases.

I don't ever remember eating alone with my parents or grandparents; friends and family members were always dropping by. One of my grandmother's sisters, the widowed Tante Marie, was a frequent guest. I nicknamed her *le cafard* ("the black cockroach") because she was always dressed in black, her hennaed hair pulled tight into a chignon, a cigarette hanging from the corner of her mouth. She would skitter around the house like the enormous cockroaches that haunted the bathrooms and scared me every morning. Her husband, it was rumored, had had many mistresses, and when he died several years after they were married, Tante Marie had been quite relieved to be left comfortably off with her four children. French was the family's common language. Arabic was used to address the servants, but when my grandmother and Tante Marie were gossiping together about other family members, they spoke Ladino—the corrupted Spanish-Hebrew of the

Middle Eastern Jews—which saved my innocent ears from scandalous stories.

A few weeks after our arrival, my grandmother hired a young Arab girl, Aishe, to take care of me. Aishe must have been about fourteen, was rather small and thin, and was always dressed in long, flowing skirts that she insisted my grandmother buy for her. Very quickly we became inseparable. Aishe washed me, dressed me, and took me for walks along the Nile. We often sat on a bench to look at the *felouks* (sailboats) passing by. Sometimes we went for an ice cream or a mango juice before returning home, where Aishe and I played endless games of lotto. Although Aishe was only an adolescent and I was barely five, she allowed me an early glimpse of the predicaments of womanhood. One afternoon, as I ran into my bedroom, I saw Aishe draped over my bed, sobbing. Horrified, I called out to my grandmother, who came rushing in. "Did you break anything? Tell me, girl! Stop crying and tell me what's wrong!" she insisted. Aishe explained that a messenger had come from her father saying that he had chosen a husband for her and that in a week's time she had to leave Cairo for her village. I looked at my grandmother's face and saw her piercing eyes still directed at Aishe. I started to cry. "Stop you two!" my grandmother yelled. "Now, Aishe, why are you crying? You don't want to leave Colette? Are you afraid of this man your father chose? Do you know him?" At every question, Aishe shook her head. Curious to know what my grandmother would ask next, I stopped crying. Aishe looked at me, then at my grandmother, then back at me, blushing and cowering slightly. She told us both, in a rapid whisper, that she was no longer a virgin, that her father would kill her if he found out, and that she didn't want to leave me.

I didn't understand what "virgin" meant but was sure it was something terrible and started to cry all over again. My grandmother sighed. "Leave it to me," she said, rolling her eyes. For the next two days, she and Tante Marie huddled together in the living room, whispering and arguing. On the third morning, my grandmother called Aishe in and told her that Waleed, the ice cream man whom Aishe liked, was willing to marry her if she was a virgin and that Tante Marie had found a way around that problem. A letter from my grandfather was sent to Aishe's father explaining that he had found her a richer husband and that the wedding would take place in Cairo. The wedding ceremony, organized by my grandmother, was brief and discreet, and Aishe continued to care for me. When I was ten, however, Aishe left to live with her husband in his hometown near the Suez Canal, but not before she told me what Tante Marie's unorthodox solution to that problem had been. A small quail egg, emptied of its contents and filled with chicken blood, had been inserted into Aishe's vagina a few hours before the wedding. Her husband was never the wiser, and she was spared a lifetime of humiliation.

I grew up fast from other relationships as well. My father, after all, was an invalid, paralyzed from the waist down and blind, and spent most of his time in his bedroom, cared for by a strong, tall Sudanese male nurse named Mustafa. I was fascinated by Mustafa's face, which had three long slashes on each cheek. Mustafa told me he had gotten the scars in a sword fight in the desert. Years later, when I asked my grandfather, he laughed and told me the scars had been made as part of Mustafa's tribe's initiation rite. When I visited my father in his room, which was often, he would be sitting in his wheelchair by the window. I would jump on his knees, and he would hold me for a short while with his good arm, then let me slide off to the floor, where I would linger for a few minutes before running off to play, only to come back an hour later. He was also my shield when I was about to be scolded by my mother. I'd bury my head in his neck and whimper, "I have done nothing! Maman is going to beat me!" He'd always reassure me with the same words: "No one is going to hurt my little girl."

My father never scolded me except once, and although I was six at the time, I remembered it because it was the only time I saw him angry with me. Once a year, men would come to clean and refurbish the oriental rugs. The rugs would be taken outside in the back garden and beaten with a bamboo paddle, the dust flying in all directions; once they were clean and dry, the men would dip a cloth in colored water and painstakingly go over the carpets' intricate designs. I decided to try this technique myself. I took my box of watercolors and started to paint my grandparents' best carpet in the living room and nearly ruined it. My mother caught me at my work (before I did irreversible damage) and shook me by the arm, screaming that I was a monster. I twisted myself free and ran to my father's room. But this time my mother followed me and told my father what I had done. My father's stern voice astonished me; he pushed me away and told me to go to my room until dinner time. I threw myself on my bed and cried myself to sleep. When I awoke, I crept back to his room with a handful of pistachios for him. He held me tightly, as if he had forgotten my crime. I watched him eat the tiny, salty, perfumed pistachios in silence, wishing that he might spring up from his chair and dance with me in his arms, the way I'd seen my uncle dance with his daughter.

A handsome, rich French beauty in her late twenties, my mother became one of the darlings of Cairo's *haute societé* and a member of the Sporting Club, a private, exclusive club in Zamaleck (a residential neighborhood across the Nile from Garden City), where she went every morning for a game of tennis or a swim, hobnobbing with the posh set and officers of the English army, then occupying Cairo. On the days I had no school, my mother sometimes took me along and taught me how to swim. Lunch would be served on the terrace that overlooked the pool. In one corner older men would sit, sipping Turkish coffee, gin and tonic, or beer while surveying the parade below of young women in their bathing suits. My mother and I would sit near the bar, joined soon after by several of her young admirers. I knew then she would let me order whatever I liked in order to distract me. At home we only ate pita bread or French bread, so I usually asked for a tomato and olive sandwich on toasted white bread drizzled with pungent olive oil. Sometimes I ordered cucumber sandwiches, wet and crisp as only the English know how to prepare them, served with mounds of golden-brown sweet potato chips, another one of my favorites. I would slowly sip my lemon soda, trying to understand the grown-up conversations. In late afternoon, my mother would go shopping with her friends or play cards in the club's cool gardens. I would be sent home alone with the chauffeur and not see her until dinner.

Although my father's mind was sharp for the next two years his health slowly deteriorated. When his condition worsened, my mother and grandfather decided that she should take my father to Aswan, in Upper Egypt. Doctors had told my mother that the region's dry heat would improve his health. They left with a whole retinue, and soon news came back that my father was getting better and that he had actually started to walk again. Meanwhile, I had started school at the French *lycée* my cousins attended. Every morning, we'd all tumble down to the two cars waiting for us; my cousins would entertain me during the short trip, telling jokes, gossiping, and giving me candy. They would stay in school for lunch, but I returned home to eat.

I dreamt of the day when I, too, would be given a lunchbox. That day arrived in September, the month when nets were stretched between houses to catch the tiny sparrows flying south from Europe. The birds, a coveted delicacy, were plucked and broiled whole on skewers, to be savored at noon or for a light supper. In the *lycée*, lunch was eaten in the courtyard. I opened my box, picked up a sparrow by its leg, and was about to put it to my mouth when an eagle swooped down, grabbed the bird in its beak, and flew away. The eagle frightened me so deeply that I refused to have lunch in school for the rest of the year, and remained the only first-grader to be picked up and taken home for the midday meal.

Six months after she had left for Aswan, my mother returned alone and, taking me in her arms, told me that my father had died. I was only seven and my mother had just turned thirty. The next few months were lonely ones. I spent most of my time in my grandmother's company, seldom seeing my mother. Several months later, my mother left Cairo, this time for Alexandria, which she found more "European." Later still, she traveled to Lebanon for long period of time to "forget." I did not see her for the next three years and often wondered if she cared for me at all, although I enjoyed the romantic and rather tragic status of "orphan," my mother not "counting" in the eyes of my family. My father had left a will that made his parents and Oncle Clément (my father's younger brother) my guardians, stating that my mother was too young to be burdened with children alone. My grandparents, who objected to my mother's busy social life, felt that my father had not trusted my mother to take care of me, and I was raised in a household dominated by a mix of cultural forces unique to the Cairo of the 1940s.

As was typical among Egyptian Jews, my grandfather was the apparent head of the household, but even as a young child, I noticed that my grandmother had an uncanny way of suggesting ideas or solutions as if they had come from my grandfather. While my grandfather was in the house, my grandmother always deferred to him, but as soon as he left, my grandmother, strong willed and dominating, took over any problem that the family had. Thus I learned very young—by observing the womenfolk—that I could make my grandfather do whatever I wanted. All I had to do was kiss him, tell him how much I loved him, shake my head full of curls, and gaze up with enormous moist eyes.

I had free reign to roam up and down the staircase, going from one apartment to another, and especially from one kitchen to another, to breathe in the smells of glorious cooking and to spy on each floor's domestic situation. There were heated arguments and whispered conversations to overhear: Tante Fortuné fought with her daughter Alice over her choice of boyfriends; Great-Aunt Becca complained to my grandmother about her husband's nightly gambling at the poker table; Tante Becca's son Vita bemoaned his bachelorhood but was loathe to marry the fat, homely heiress his parents had chosen for him. I would find him sitting in the back garden, smoking a cigar and utterly dejected. As if I were his peer, he'd turn to me and moan, "I hate her. I don't want to marry her . . . What shall I do?" He ended up marrying her anyway, simply to offset his father's debts.

Like the tides, the rhythms of our home were repeated each day. In the early morning and late evening, the household would revolve around my grandfather Vita. When leaving in the morning for the offices of the department store he owned—dressed in a three-piece European suit, with a traditional red felt *tarboosh* on his head and a gold watchchain stretched across his round belly—he looked both stern and self-satisfied. My grandmother would follow him to the door, a glass of water in her hand. Grandpère would cross the threshold, walk five steps, turn around and reenter the house. My grandmother would hand him the glass of water, which he would drain; then he'd bend down to kiss her before leaving again, this time for the day. "To ward off the evil spirits and be sure he will come back safe," my grandmother would explain. She would repeatedly remind me of the most important of these superstitions: *Pull your left ear three times if a black cat or an albino child crosses your path* (I never saw an albino child in the twelve years I spent in Cairo!). And, *Spit three times to prevent the evil eye if someone tells you you are beautiful, or if a hearse crosses your path, or if you are afraid of something or someone.* I am amazed that today my left ear lobe is not twice as long as my right from pulling it so often. Spitting three times when fate has been challenged has become my own family's habit.

My grandfather's department store was in a populated neighborhood near the Khan-al-Khalili central market. On Fridays he would only work in the morning, and sometimes I would accompany him to the store. I loved going with him. We would first stop in front of the store's main entrance, where an old beggar crouched on the sidewalk. My grandfather gave me some coins to drop in the man's cup. "You must always give to people poorer than you," he would say. We would then go in, and I would be sent to the toy department, where I could play with all the toys. My favorite was a large rubber doll, nearly as tall as I was. It had blond hair and was dressed in a frilly party dress. I loved that doll and was always afraid it would be sold, but Friday after Friday, like a best friend, it was there waiting for me. I would talk to her and tell her stories, often having a very elaborate dialogue, providing both questions and answers. Perhaps my grandfather had given orders to the staff not to sell the doll, and he gave it to me for my sixth birthday. From that day, it lay in a corner of my room, untouched.

The Khan-al-Khalili open-air market consisted of winding streets and narrow, dark alleys lined with stalls. Streets were named after what was sold on them: Gold Street, Copper and Brass Streets, Silk and Cotton Streets, Carpet Street. At lunchtime, merchants sitting on stools outside their open stores greeted my grandfather loudly in Arabic. He, in turn, inquired about their health or their family. Often he would bring a bolt of cloth from his store as a present for someone's daughter who was getting married. My grandfather loved Egyptian food, especially street food, like *ful medames*, the traditional Egyptian dish of stewed brown fava beans, and he was a regular at Aboushakra, a tiny restaurant located near Gold Street. Its walls, vaguely illuminated by exposed bulbs, had been painted pink years before and were now faded to an indescribable color. There were long tables covered with paper tablecloths and surrounded by cane chairs. As we entered, the owner greeted him loudly, *"Ahlen wha haslen Pacha!"* ("Welcome,

Pasha!"). Quickly a table would be cleaned and set for us. On Fridays, with ritual-like fervor, we began our meal with hot *ta'miyya*—a falafel made with broad beans—spicy, moist, and dark green inside and crisp on the outside, covered with roasted sesame seeds. These were served with fresh, toasted pita and a tomato salad mixed with sliced red onions in vinai-

TA'MIYYA

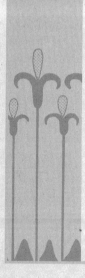

Peeled, split fava beans for this Egyptian falafel are available in most Italian or Middle Eastern grocery stores. *Ta'miyya* is served with *tehina*.

SOAK ½ POUND OF peeled, split dried fava beans in water to cover generously overnight.

THE NEXT DAY, drain the beans and place in a food processor with 1 chopped garlic clove and purée until ground. Add ¾ cup chopped parsley; the green tops of ½ bunch scallions, chopped; ½ teaspoon ground cumin; ½ teaspoon baking powder; ½ teaspoon salt; and 1 tablespoon chopped fresh cilantro. Pulse and process until thoroughly ground and the mixture comes together. Turn out into a bowl, wet your hands, and form into 2-inch balls. Flatten each ball slightly and roll in toasted sesame seeds. Place on a pan, cover, and refrigerate until you are ready to fry.

HEAT 2 INCHES OF vegetable oil in a saucepan to 365 degrees. Drop a few *ta'miyya* into the oil and fry until golden brown, 5 to 8 minutes. Drain on paper towels and serve with *tehina* as an appetizer. Or stuff them with chopped lettuce and *tehina* into pita for lunch. This makes about 24.

grette. We then enjoyed an order of grilled, tender beef *kofta*—meatballs on skewers. Pink and green ceramic bowls of *tehina*—a lemony sesame sauce—and a dish of pickled vegetables graced every table. I was very fond of these garlicky

TEHINA

PLACE ½ CUP SESAME PASTE in the bowl of a food processor with 1 cup water, the juice of 2 lemons, 4 chopped garlic cloves, and 1 teaspoon ground cumin. Pulse to combine, then process until the mixture has the consistency of thick cream. Transfer to a bowl and add salt to taste. *Tehina* will keep for at least a week, tightly covered in the refrigerator.

pickles, ate too many of them, and invariably ended up with a stomachache. My grandmother would rail against my grandfather as soon as we returned home: "How can you let her eat so much? You know she always gets sick!" He would promise to be more vigilant, of course, but would continue to indulge me every Friday.

At home in the evenings my grandfather would sit on the front terrace, watching the sunset, swishing a horsetail flyswatter from side to side. This was the hour when the entire extended family would join him, gossiping, munching on pistachios or roasted melon seeds, dipping bread in pungent *babaghanou* or *tarama salat*. The younger crowd drank beer or the gin and tonics that the English had made fashionable since the beginning of the war. My grandfather never drank any alcohol, just fruit juices. My cousins and I would play games, or

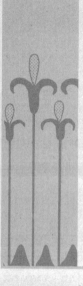

BABAGHANOU

In Egypt, eggplant was roasted over hot coals until the skin was charred. At home, I char the eggplant directly over the gas flame, turning frequently with tongs until the juices begin to ooze out. It can also be baked in a 425-degree oven for 30 minutes.

CHAR 2 LARGE EGGPLANTS over gas flames until soft, then allow to cool. Peel the eggplants and let them drain in a sieve. Purée the eggplant in a food processor with I tablespoon fresh lemon juice, I tablespoon ground cumin, I chopped garlic clove, I $\frac{1}{2}$ tablespoons olive oil, and salt and pepper to taste.

TRANSFER TO A BOWL and stir in I tablespoon finely chopped parsley. Add I cup *tehina* if you like. This makes about 2 cups without the *tehina*, 3 cups with.

I would curl up on my grandfather's lap, listening to everyone's chatter. Around eight, as the smell of roasting pigeons mixed with cumin and lime began to waft through the house, my grandmother would shoo her children and other grandchildren out, and everyone would return to their own apartments for dinner, except the two or three guests that had just happened to drop in or that my grandfather had invited for that night.

The table was set with a white damask tablecloth; in the center, two silver birds seemed ready to take off, their feathers realistically etched. The cutlery was heavy ornate silver, and the dishes were white porcelain with silver rims (the gold-rimmed Limoges plates and Baccarat wine glasses were used only for very special occasions). Osman, our servant, dressed in a white *galabeyya* (the traditional long white cotton robe) with a red sash, was silent as he served dinner.

Grandpère, a great eater, was always very interested in the dinner menu, discussing at length with my grandmother the virtues of a dish, its spices, and how well Ahmet, the cook, had prepared it. He liked stews; she preferred roasts. He adored grilled chitterlings; she disliked them intensely and would not allow Ahmet to make them. He loved stuffed eggplant and green peppers; she delighted in stuffed zucchini or okra cooked with tomatoes and onions. She relished squab stuffed with rice and pine nuts; he wanted them grilled and spiced with lime and cumin. He would eat three or four at one sitting, picking up the squab leg delicately with two fingers. "Pick them up with your fingers too, Colette," he would say to me. "You cannot use a fork and a knife to eat these birds." My grandmother would frown, muttering that this was very undignified for *une jeune fille de bonne famille*, but I would attack my squab with gusto. Often Grandpère and I would compare the number of bones left on our plates.

Desserts were the only part of the meal about which my grandfather and I did not agree. I never liked sweets, and he thrived on them. He liked the heavy, honey-soaked *baklava* served with *eishta*, heavy cream made from water buffalo milk. The rich cream was spread on a piece of marble, allowed to set, folded several times and thickly sliced. He would lick his lips at each bite and grunt with pleasure. He also liked French desserts like soufflés and crème caramel, which Ahmet made so well. But I did share his love of mangoes, and when mangoes were in season, Grandpère would go every two weeks to

STUFFED SQUAB

CHOOSE 4 OF THE SMALLEST SQUAB you can find (in Egypt they were smaller than quail), and allow one per person. Begin the night before by soaking $\frac{1}{2}$ pound hulled wheat kernels in water to cover.

REMOVE THE GIZZARD, heart, and neck from the cavity and snip off the wings of 4 squab. Bring 1 quart of water to a boil in a saucepan, add the parts, turn off the heat, and let sit for 10 minutes. Drain and cool. Cut the gizzard and heart into small pieces, and remove as much meat as possible from the neck and wings. Set the meat aside.

RINSE THE SQUAB in cold water and dry well. Heat 2 tablespoons vegetable oil in a skillet, add 2 minced onions, and sauté for 3 minutes. Add the reserved meat and sauté another 3 minutes. Remove from the heat. Drain the wheat kernels and add to the onions along with 1 teaspoon ground cinnamon and salt and pepper to taste. Stuff the squab with this mixture and tie the legs together with kitchen string.

TIE 4 ONIONS in a piece of cheesecloth with 3 cardamom seeds and 2 bay leaves. Bring 3 quarts of water to a boil in a large pot. Add the cheesecloth bag and salt and pepper. Add the squab, bring back to a boil, then lower the heat and simmer for 45 minutes. Remove the squab from the broth and pat dry.

HEAT $\frac{1}{4}$ CUP vegetable oil in a skillet. Fry the squab on all sides until golden brown. Arrange on

[CONTINUED]

a platter and keep warm. Remove the onions from the cheesecloth and purée in a food processor. Place in a saucepan with $1\frac{1}{2}$ cups of the broth, 2 tablespoons fresh lemon juice, and salt and pepper to taste. Bring to a boil and cook over high heat for 4 minutes. Place in a sauceboat and serve with the squab.

the mango market. He knew the sellers well, and once there, would plop himself on a wooden crate and discuss the different types offered for sale. He preferred the large, fat ones with their overwhelming sweet smell to the long, flat Indian mangoes. Once he had tasted several, he would order a case, and we would be served mangoes every night. By the end of the first week, my grandfather would start to become impatient for Ahmet to tell him that the mangoes had become overripe and that he needed to turn them into a rich mousse—my grandfather's favorite dessert. Grandmother, always the moralist, would whine, "I told you not to buy a whole case. Mangoes don't keep!"

CHAPTER 3

Ahmet and Grandmaman

I AM IN THE KITCHEN PREPARING DINNER, TESTING a recipe for an article about beans. *Ful medamas* simmers in a saucepan, releasing a familiar nutlike scent in its steam. The front doorbell rings urgently, announcing my nine-year-old grandson Matthew. He runs toward me. "Hi, Grandmaman! It's smells good . . . I'm starving. Can we cook?" He helps me prepare the lemon vinaigrette that will grace the brown fava beans, warm, partially mashed, and stuffed in a fresh pita. Since Matthew was born, the bond between us has been uncannily

FUL MEDAMES

This dish is traditionally cooked overnight and can be made with canned Egyptian small fava beans. Egyptian pickles are a mix of turnips, onions, and hot peppers and are available in Middle Eastern groceries.

COVER I POUND dried Egyptian fava beans with water and soak overnight. The next day, drain the beans and place in a large saucepan with I head of garlic, cut in half. Add 7 cups of water and bring to a boil. Lower to a simmer, add 6 eggs in their shells, the juice of a lemon, and salt and pepper to taste. Cook the beans for I2 hours, or until tender, checking occasionally and adding water if needed.

PREPARE 6 INDIVIDUAL BOWLS. Place I tablespoon chopped scallion, I tablespoon olive oil, $\frac{1}{2}$ tablespoon lemon juice, and salt and pepper into each bowl. Peel the eggs and place one in each bowl. Spoon in the *ful* and serve with Egyptian pickles and toasted pita. This is enough for 6.

strong. Soon after my daughter Marianne gave birth to him, she and I signed a contract to write a cookbook together. When the book was near completion, we had to test and photograph the recipes. Matthew was ten months old at the time, so we placed his little chair right on the kitchen counter as we worked. I'd put a bit of whatever I was cooking on a spoon, waft it under his nose, and ask him if he liked it. Marianne would invariably grumble, "He's too young . . . he doesn't know!" but his smile told me the contrary. At three, he'd sniff the fresh tarragon that I'd rub between my fingers; at four, he learned how to scramble eggs, standing next to me on a stepladder; at five, he was trusted with a knife. I had murmured that I needed to peel some garlic, and Matthew piped up, "Oh, let me . . . let me!" My French grandmother had refused to let me cut or peel anything, and to this day I often cut myself when wielding a knife. I succumbed to his pleas and was amazed at how adept he was once I guided his hand, which held a small utility knife, over the first clove. I showed him how to rub a halved clove over stale French bread to toss in the salad bowl; how to mix olive oil, lemon juice, salt, pepper, and herbs; and how to taste the dressing with a salad leaf. That day, his favorite word became *delicious*. Marianne walked into the kitchen and stared at the counter in disbelief. There was olive oil dripping from it, and cut lemons and garlic cloves strewn everywhere. Matthew's face, hands, and hair were sticky, and his shirt was stained. "You smell of garlic. Go wash your hands!" she said with a half-smile—my own mother's words haunting me across a generation.

Matthew's presence transports me back to the Cairo kitchen, where I am tasting the *ful* that Ahmet, the cook, prepared and helping Grandmaman Marguerite mix dough while she sings songs to me in Arabic. Her family pride was profoundly linked to the kitchen, so when I attempted to make *sambusaks* once for my friends and did not follow her recipe for this cheese-filled golden dough faithfully, she was outraged. "This recipe is at least hundreds of years old. You do not change it!" she shouted. I see her standing at the stove, a diminutive woman usually dressed in black. Her thick, curly, henna-dyed hair was pulled upward in a large chignon; there

SAMBUSAKS

TO MAKE THE PASTRY combine ½ cup melted butter, ½ cup vegetable oil, ½ cup hot water, and a pinch of salt. Stir in 2 cups flour. Turn out onto a floured board and work in another cup of flour. Knead until the dough holds together; it will be soft. Shape into a ball, wrap in plastic, and refrigerate for 30 minutes.

FOR THE FILLING, place ⅔ pound crumbled feta, 2 tablespoons grated parmesan cheese, 2 eggs, 4 teaspoons baking powder, and pepper to taste in the bowl of a food processor. Pulse until light and creamy.

DIVIDE THE DOUGH into 20 balls. Flatten each ball into a 4-inch round on a floured surface. Place a heaping tablespoon of filling in the center of each round, brush the edges with water, fold over, and press the edges with a fork to seal. As you finish, place on a greased baking sheet. Brush the *sambusaks* with beaten egg, and bake in a pre-heated 375-degree oven until golden brown, about 35 minutes. Serve hot or at room temperature.

was always a lock of hair escaping that she would try, again and again and without success, to push back into her chignon. My daughter Marianne, who looks like her, has the same gesture of trying to push a lock of curly dark hair back behind her ear. I smile as I watch the curl fall down in front of her eyes.

Grandmaman spent her time trotting around the ground-floor Cairo apartment, a large set of keys dangling from her waist. The pantry was locked, and every morning she would open it to take out rice, or measure oil and sugar for the day's meal, or check on the pickled turnips and the salted garlic. She enjoyed her role of supervising the maids, cook, and chauffeur. She had a quick temper that would flair if she thought one of the servants or one of us did not listen to her. The first time I heard her sharp voice rising in anger, I ran and hid in my father's bedroom. When I told him I was afraid of my grandmother's voice, he laughed and said, "Go back in the kitchen and see what they are doing." I crept back and found my grandmother and Ahmet laughing together at something Aishe had said. From that day on, I knew that Grandmaman was a kind, gentle woman with a fist of iron.

Grandmaman was a superb cook. She reigned in the kitchen, but she had to share power with Ahmet. Every morning they waged battles. Ahmet, a short, wiry Sudanese, had been with my grandparents since he was twenty-five. He had married young and by the age of eighteen had three children. The village was very poor, and Ahmet, having no work, had left his wife and children to seek his fortune in Cairo. He had entered into service in the house of a French diplomat, a friend of my aunt Fortuné, as a manservant. Very quickly he had graduated to the kitchen, as an assistant to the French chef. A born cook, Ahmet soon learned the elaborate French dishes preferred in that house. When the diplomat returned to France, Tante Fortuné asked my grandfather to take Ahmet into our household. By the time I arrived in Egypt, Ahmet had been entrenched in the kitchen for perhaps fifteen years. He was stubborn, but very kind, and loved the children in our large household as much as he missed his. I was the only child who wanted to be with him in the kitchen, especially when Grandmaman was not looking, and he and I became especially close. Grandmaman and Ahmet argued every morning with great shouts. (I was always afraid that Ahmet would get so angry that he'd leave me like all the people I loved.) He would propose a whole fish in aspic, a tarragon-stuffed roast chicken, a ballottine of duck, or his famous gigot—pink, tender, and stuffed with garlic. Grandmaman, however, loved all things Egyptian. Her idea of a meal might begin, for example, with *mulukhiyya* (a delicate Egyptian soup made with the green herb of the same name) served over white Egyptian rice, then continue with fried fish with *cousbareia* sauce or roast chicken on a bed of leeks. Grandmaman was a great believer in the restora-

MULUKHIYYA

Mulukhiyya is a rather bitter herb with a natural thickening agent. It cannot be found fresh in the United States but is available dried or frozen in stores selling Middle Eastern products.

BRING 5 CUPS OF CHICKEN STOCK to a boil in a saucepan. Add two 1-pound packages *mulukhiyya*, reduce the heat, and simmer for 5 to 10 minutes to dissolve the herb.

HEAT 3 TABLESPOONS OLIVE OIL in a small skillet over medium heat. Add 4 minced garlic cloves and cook for 2 to 3 minutes. Stir in 2 tablespoons ground coriander and 1 tablespoon ground cumin, cook for 2 minutes, then add the mixture to the stock. Stir in the juice of 2 lemons and salt and pepper to taste. Simmer the soup for 8 minutes.

DIVIDE 1 CUP COOKED long-grain rice among 8 bowls, ladle the soup over the rice, and serve.

FRIED FISH WITH COUSBAREIA SAUCE

PAT 2 POUNDS OF cleaned butterfish or mullet (or any firm-fleshed fish) dry with paper towels. Season 2 cups of flour with salt and pepper and dredge the fish in it. Heat 2 cups olive oil in a deep skillet and when the oil is very hot, fry the fish quickly over high heat for about 6 minutes until golden brown. Drain on paper towels.

HEAT 2 TABLESPOONS OLIVE OIL in a separate skillet. Add 2 thinly sliced onions and sauté until soft and golden brown. Then add 2 cups of peeled, seeded, and diced tomatoes; 1 cup chopped hazelnuts; and ½ cup roasted and chopped pine nuts. Cook for 4 minutes. Add ½ cup water and ½ cup chopped parsley, season with salt and pepper, and cook for 5 minutes. Add the fish to the sauce and simmer for 10 minutes, adding more water if the sauce becomes too thick. This is enough for 4 and should be served with rice.

tive power of leeks. She would recommend leeks to my teenage cousin Renée, who was complaining of being too fat. "Eat only leeks for one day," she would say in her imperative tone of voice, "and you will be slim." She told Zaki, my eighteen-year-old cousin, to eat leeks to heal his acne, and would insist that I eat them at least twice a week so that I might sing in tune like my other cousins. We never saw any results, but we continued to listen to her and eat leeks.

Ahmet went shopping daily. Once a week, however, Grandmaman took charge. Once a week, on Fridays, she would call

ROAST CHICKEN ON A BED OF LEEKS

WIPE A 5-POUND CHICKEN dry with paper towels. Mix 2 tablespoons olive oil with 1 tablespoon lemon juice, 2 tablespoons fresh tarragon, and salt and pepper. Rub the chicken inside and out with this mixture.

REMOVE THE OUTER LEAVES from 2 pounds of leeks and wash well. Finely chop 2 of the leeks and carefully slide under the skin of the chicken. Cut the remaining leeks into 1-inch pieces, place in a roasting pan, season with salt and pepper, and dot with 2 tablespoons butter. Place the chicken on top of the leeks, add 3 cups chicken broth, and roast in a preheated 375-degree oven for 1 hour and 30 minutes, or until golden brown and cooked through. Check from time to time and add water if the leeks are drying out.

CARVE THE CHICKEN into serving pieces and place on a platter. Stir the leeks (being sure to scrape the bottom of the pan) and add up to $\frac{1}{2}$ cup chicken stock to make a sauce. Taste for salt and pepper and spoon over the chicken. This dish is delicious with French lentils and a salad, and is enough for 4 to 6.

for the horse-drawn carriage to take her to the city's main market, accompanied by Abdullah, Ahmet's son, to carry her purchases. If school were not in session, I'd join them. I'd sit primly next to Grandmaman on the red velveteen seats of the shiny black carriage, and she'd sing me a song in Arabic about a horse and a young damsel in distress. I heard the song so many times that I can still sing it today, although probably out of tune despite all the leeks I've eaten.

The open market was located in a large street, at the end of which was an enclosed fish and poultry market. The carriage would drop us at the corner, and Grandmaman would lead the way into the dusty, noisy, crowded market. We would first stop at a vegetable store, where Hassan, the owner, would greet her with flowery words. The vegetables were displayed on shelves, and Hassan would be perched on the very top, looking down on his customers while shouting orders to his helper. As I marveled at the abundant displays of fruit and vegetables, Grandmaman bought small young okra, intensely red tomatoes, zucchini, and cucumbers, choosing perfect specimens quickly and expertly. When it came to eggplant, she'd take much more time; she was famous for her *babaghanou* and took this vegetable very seriously. The eggplant had to be plump, deep purple, not too large, but not small either. She touched, tapped, and weighed, arguing endlessly with Hassan before buying.

The watermelon stand was next. The watermelons were stacked on a cart, the small ones in front and the larger ones in the back The seller knew my grandmother and was always prepared for her. As soon as he saw her coming, he would reach for a watermelon and tell her that he had selected it specially for her. With a dramatic gesture, he'd pick up a large knife and make a cone incision, removing the piece with a flourish and handing it to her, superlatives flowing. Every week my grandmother fell for it, and Abdullah would be handed the largest watermelon and nearly collapse under its weight. Grandmaman would then send Abdullah back to the carriage to drop off some of our purchases. Invariably she berated poor Abdullah for taking too long to return. Abdullah would roll his eyes, look at me, and then burst out laughing, knowing that Grandmaman would give him a *backshish* at the end of the day for all his pains.

We would then proceed to the poultry and meat market. Grandmaman always started with the pigeon seller. As soon as she appeared, someone would bring her an old padded wooden chair to sit on while a young boy would be sent to get her some strong, overly sweet Arab coffee, which would be served in a tiny porcelain cup set on a bright silver tray. She would sip her coffee while discussing the quality of the pigeons shown to her. "The birds had better be tender and plump," she'd warn, squeezing the poor bird's breast, "because they weren't the last time!" The pigeons were then killed, plucked, and handed to Abdullah, without being wrapped in greasy newspaper, which was a common practice. Abdullah always carried a special cloth bag for the poultry.

After the pigeons, we would visit the chicken seller. The store my grandmother liked to shop in was always crowded with women wrapped in black from head to toe, arguing about prices or how fat the chickens or the hens were. My grandmother would insist that the hen be filled with unborn eggs, that the chicken be plump, and that the vendor—brandishing the selected bird by its feet—not kill it in front of me.

The next step was the meat market, which I despised. I'd close my eyes and hide in my grandmother's skirts because I did not want to look at the baby goats and young lambs, skinned and hanging by their feet, looking very dead, or at the large slab of beef on the marble counter. Grandmaman would ask for thin slices of beef, insisting that it should be cut from the leg. She would tap her thighs with the flat of her hand making a smacking noise as if to underline her words. The slices had to be cut thin as the beef was often quite tough. I never had a steak until I went back to Paris and had my first juicy *rôti de boeuf* (roast beef). The worst moment was when she stopped to buy slices of beef liver—large, red, and bloody—that made me feel sick. Even today I cannot eat cooked liver except if I choose hot foie gras in a restaurant. We then stopped at a dried fruit and nut store, one of my favorites, especially in the fall, when the fresh pistachios were available. These pistachios were covered with an easy-to-remove thin red skin, and their meat was tender and bright green. I also loved to pick at the different pepitas (seeds). There were at least ten different varieties of pepitas—some small, like the melon seeds, and some very large, like the sunflower seeds. My grandmother would buy some of each, to be served at six o'clock on the terrace with the drinks. Then she would choose fat, rich dried apricots from Turkey, pitted prunes from Syria, and tiny dried raisins from Ismir.

Having concluded all her shopping, Grandmaman would rapidly trot back to the carriage, oblivious of poor Abdullah, laden again with all her purchases, who could barely follow her. Returning home from her shopping, Grandmaman would triumphantly display all her purchases to Ahmet, who would mumble that she had paid too much for the the squab or the fish, or that the watermelon was overripe. Grandmaman would sniff once or twice, order *lahma mahshiya* (thin slices of marinated beef stuffed with Kashkaval cheese and onions and baked) for dinner, and sail out of the kitchen to join my aunts on the terrace. There they would nibble on *lukoum*—chewy, pistachio-filled sweets—while Grandmaman recounted her morning's adventures. As the sun set, a wonderful aroma,

LAHMA MASHSHIYA

ASK THE BUTCHER to slice 2 pounds of beef round very thin, and pound the slices. Mix ½ cup finely chopped parsley, 2 tablespoons grated *Kashkaval* cheese, 2 tablespoons grated dry goat cheese, and freshly ground black pepper. Spread the mixture on the slices of beef, roll tight, and tie with kitchen string.

MIX 2 FINELY CHOPPED ONIONS, 3 minced garlic cloves, ½ teaspoon grated nutmeg, I tablespoon lemon juice, and I cup beef bouillon in a large bowl. Add the beef rolls and set aside to marinate for 2 hours.

REMOVE THE MEAT from the marinade, and brown well in a skillet with I tablespoon oil. Transfer the rolls to a casserole when done. Add another tablespoon of oil to the skillet and stir in ¼ cup flour. Cook, stirring constantly, for 2 minutes. Add the marinade and ½ cup beef bouillon, bring to a boil, and cook over low heat for 3 minutes. Pour the sauce over the beef and bake in a preheated 325-degree oven for 20 minutes. This will serve 4 people.

sweet and pungent, would slowly filter to the terrace, and I would run to the kitchen, impatient, asking Ahmet how soon we were to have dinner. To appease my hunger, Ahmet would stuff a pita bread with cold *kobeiba* patties (chopped meatballs) and shoo me out of the kitchen.

I spent a lot of time with Ahmet in the kitchen despite my grandmother's admonition that this was not the place for *une*

KOBEIBA

This is a Lebanese and Syrian dish in which the meat is pounded in a large stone mortar until tender.

COVER 1 POUND BULGUR with water and soak for 20 minutes. Dice 2 pounds beef round and pound until tender in a large, heavy mortar.

COMBINE THE BEEF, 2 finely chopped onions, ¼ cup finely chopped chicken fat, 2 tablespoons pine nuts, and salt and pepper in a bowl. Mix well.

IN ANOTHER BOWL combine 2 pounds chopped lamb, 2 grated onions, 2 tablespoons lemon juice, and salt and pepper. Mix well.

WITH WET HANDS, take a piece of the beef mixture. Place it in one palm and with your index finger make a hole in the center, pushing the beef out onto your palm to make a thin layer. Fill the hole halfway with some of the lamb. Moisten your hand again, close the beef around the lamb, and form a ball. Continue until you have used up all the meat.

HEAT 2 TABLESPOONS OIL in a large skillet. Fry the *kobeiba* until golden brown and cooked through. Drain on paper towels and serve hot with pita or Egyptian fried rice. This is plenty for 6.

jeune fille de bonne famille. The kitchen was very large, with two windows overlooking the back garden. There was a wide, deep stone sink with a copper faucet, and a large counter with bowls of limes and lemons and jars of spices. On the floor near the window were "primus" kerosene burners on which most of the cooking was done. A large refrigerator dominated the corner of the kitchen, and on the opposite corner was a large gas oven for baking. Near the counter were a couple of high stools where I would often sit watching Ahmet prepare lunch or dinner, or just put up pickles for the family.

Many of the ingredients used in cooking were made up in quantity by Ahmet. Crushed garlic, for example, was prepared once a year. Aishe, Osman (the valet), and Ahmet would all sit outside in the garden and peel pounds of fresh harvested garlic, which they crushed and minced with salt, then stored in glass jars with a tight lid. The jars sat on the counter amid other jars of black sesame seeds, coriander seeds, and cumin seeds. Small, fresh, aromatic mint was brought in from the market once every two months. After rinsing the mint several times, Ahmet would spread the leaves on sheets of newspaper to dry in the sun. This would take about a week. He would then pick the dried leaves from the stems and rub them between the palms of his hands to crush the mint into powder. He'd open his hands and allow me to smell the strong, sweet aroma of the crushed mint. The powder would be put through a fine sieve before being stored in a glass jar. He used the mint in chicken soup and lentil stew. I loved to be in the kitchen in the fall, when Ahmet prepared *ful nabe*, dried broad beans. He would soak some of the beans in an earthenware container for four to six days, changing the water every twelve hours, until the beans had germinated and the sprouts were at least an inch high. He'd offer me the sprouts on a piece of toasted pita, drizzled with olive oil and sprinkled with salt. He boiled the remaining beans and served them cold as an appetizer. The outside skin of the bean is tough and inedible, so Ahmet taught me how to bite one end and squeeze the inner bean right into my mouth.

Ahmet cooked a different meal from ours for the servants. A large *idras* (a large copper vessel that rests on its side) of fragrant *ful medames* was perpetually warming on one of the stoves. In my house, *ful* was only meant for the staff, yet because I was passionate about it, Ahmet, risking my grandmother's ire, would ply me with *ful* after school instead of the *tartine* (baguette slathered with fresh butter and jam) my cousins would eat.

Every year around April, a drama would unfold in our household: Ahmet would announce that it was time for him to go to Upper Egypt and visit his wife. Life in our house would be turned upside down. I can still hear my grandmother's high-pitched voice trying to convince Ahmet that he should try not to have any more children. Ahmet would smile at her mockingly and say, *"Insha Allah!"* ("God bless!"). After all, she had had nine children of her own! My grandmother would take over the kitchen with Aishe and the chauffeur, Hassan, as her helpers. While Ahmet was away, Grandpère would invite no one for dinner. He was afraid of Grandmaman's wrath, as she would complain of how incompetent the servants were and how tired she was. Poor Aishe! Grandmaman was never happy with the way she followed her instructions. The milk would boil over. "Careful, girl!" Grandmaman would shout in Arabic. "Look at the pot, not at me!"

I, on the other hand, was quite happy because I was allowed in the kitchen to watch Grandmaman prepare her delicious *sambusaks,* and I was also allowed to knead the dough. The mixture was warm, and I loved putting my hands in the middle of it. She would roll the dough thin, cut it into rounds with a Turkish coffee cup, and create half-moons filled with the cheese stuffing. While the *sambusaks* were baking, my

MAHASHI KRONB (STUFFED CABBAGE)

This dish was developed by my grandmother and was served for special occasions.

BRING 3 QUARTS of water to boil in a large pot. Trim the stem end of a large head of cabbage and discard any torn leaves. Place the cabbage in the boiling water and cook for 10 minutes. Remove the cabbage with a slotted spoon and refresh under cold water. Drain well. Carefully pull the outer leaves back, so they lie flat but remain attached at the stem. Cut out the center leaves with a paring knife, separate them, and trim the tough center stems.

MIX TOGETHER I POUND ground lamb, 2 teaspoons cumin, I teaspoon chopped fresh sage, ¼ cup finely chopped fresh parsley, 2 minced garlic cloves, I lightly beaten egg, ¾ cup long grain rice, and salt and pepper to taste. Place I tablespoon of the lamb mixture in the center of a trimmed cabbage leaf. Fold in the sides, then roll loosely to form a small bundle. Repeat with the remaining lamb and leaves, reserving one of the larger leaves.

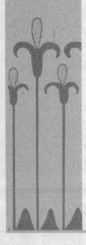

ARRANGE ABOUT ONE-THIRD of the bundles on the flattened cabbage, leaving a 4-inch border. Mound the remaining bundles on top and cover with the reserved leaf. Bring up the edges of the flattened leaves and tie the entire package together with kitchen string; it should resemble a reconstructed cabbage.

PLACE IN A LARGE, deep saucepan, add I½ cups chicken stock and ½ cup olive oil. Bring to a

[CONTINUED]

boil, reduce the heat, cover, and simmer for 25
minutes until very tender. Carefully transfer the
cabbage to a platter and cut off the string. Open
the cabbage at the table and serve with plain
yogurt. This is enough for 8 to 10.

cousins would slowly drift into the kitchen, but if
Grandmaman called upon them to help, they would all disap-
pear until the *sambusaks* were brought to the terrace. I also
helped her make stuffed cabbage, learning to stuff the
blanched leaves with the ground beef and rice and transform
them into a large cabbage. When Ahmet returned from his
trip, Grandmaman could not hide her pleasure at seeing him
again. She would greet him like an old friend, ask about his
wife and children, and then immediately order dinner. The
battle between them would resume with new ardor, and to my
grandfather's delight, the household would go back to its routine. Guests again would come to dinner, and my grandmother's complaints about being too tired stopped.

Dinner was a formal affair every night, with Grandpère sitting at the head of the table, Grandmaman to his left, and the
guest of that night to his right. The soup was served first, followed by stuffed beef or grilled *kobeiba* served with rice, a stew
of okra with tomatoes, a salad, and, for dessert, Ahmet's glorious chocolate soufflé. The rice was fluffy and delicious, but
the best part was its bottom layer, which was crisp and golden
brown. Egyptian rice is first fried in a tablespoon or two of
oil before the broth is added, and it is allowed to nearly burn
at the bottom. The stewed rice was served in a bowl, and the

crackling browned rice was served separately. I was always afraid that by the time the dish reached me there would be no more burnt rice, and I would sit at the table looking so forlorn that Grandmaman would always be sure that I got to be served first, before the other guests at the table. At the end of the meal, silver bowls filled with warm water and rose petals were placed in front of each guest to rinse their fingertips.

In 1946, Abdullah, Ahmet's oldest son, had arrived unannounced at our doorstep one summer day—a skinny twelve-year-old, shy and looking lost, with a warm smile. Grandmaman was annoyed at the idea of having a boy so young in her service. "He should be in school," she'd argue with Ahmet, "not working for me." I was then eight years old and pleased at the idea of having a new playmate. As usual, a

EGYPTIAN "FRIED" RICE

WASH 2 CUPS of short grain rice and set aside in a colander to drain.

HEAT 2 TABLESPOONS OIL in a heavy saucepan. When the oil is hot, add the rice and fry it until each grain is coated with oil. Add 3 cups hot water and salt to taste, stir, and cook uncovered over moderate heat until all the water is absorbed. Cover, reduce the heat to low, and cook for 30 minutes more. Spoon the top layer of rice into a bowl. Remove the browned layer with a spatula. You can break that layer into several pieces and top the rice with them, or serve the browned rice in a separate bowl. This will serve 6.

compromise was reach between Ahmet and Grandmaman. Every morning Abdullah would go to the local Arab school, and every afternoon he would help around the house. Abdullah became my best friend. He taught me how to ride my bicycle by holding it while I rode around and around the block, without ever complaining. Like his father, he would spoil me, climbing the mango tree to get me a mango or sneaking out of the house to buy me *zalabia*, the tiny bits of fried dough rolled in honey, from the street vendor—both treats forbidden by Grandmaman.

Almost thirty years after leaving Egypt, I finally returned to Cairo with my husband and son. Our first stop was the house in Garden City. My grandparents had long since died, and my uncles and aunts had moved away—but the house was still there. I peered through the black gate into a mostly decrepit garden and spied the flourishing mango tree. My heart beat furiously as I rang the bell. A tall, handsome Arab, wearing a long robe and a white turban around his head, appeared. In faltering Arabic I told him that I had once lived in the house with my grandparents. He suddenly tapped his fingers over his lips and made a high-pitched cry. "I am Abdullah, Ahmet's son," he explained. "You came back! I knew you would! *Al-hamd-lil-lah!* (Praise Allah!)" The next morning we met in a café, and Abdullah told me that his father had returned to his village in Upper Egypt when my grandparents died and that the house had been sold by my uncles. Abdullah had married, had two grown sons, and was now the guardian of the property. We lingered over strong coffee and shared memories of the tastes and smells of his father's kitchen.

CHAPTER 4
The Weddings

MATCHMAKING AND THE WEDDINGS THAT ENSUED
took most of my grandmother's free time.
The subject of marriage troubled the older
generations. In their eyes, too many young
people went outside the clan and married for-
eigners who would take them far away. My
father was one of these renegades, and even
my grandfather did not think that his marrying my mother—a Parisian—had been a
good idea, although her large dowry was a
point in her favor. When a young person was
about to wed a person whose family's pedigree

could not be accounted for, my grandparents would invariably exclaim, *"On ne sait pas d'ou il vient!"* ("We don't know where he comes from!") The other problem was flight abroad, even without the excuse of matrimony. Some of my cousins were going to South America—*"au bout du diable!"* ("to the end of the world!"), my grandmother would mutter, shaking her head vigorously at the idea of losing control of her brood. The imperative was to marry off sons and daughters to people you knew, so the couple would settle in Cairo or Alexandria. I found myself having a similar reaction when my youngest daughter announced that she was marrying a German and planned to live in Berlin. Without thinking, I sputtered, "But it's at the end of the world. How could you!"

I'd often eavesdrop on long telephone chats about who was seeing whom, what young woman was in need of a husband, and whether a beau was suitable or had a good (meaning rich) situation. Questions were fired from both sides of the line: How large was Huguette's dowry? Did you hear that Jacob Levi was losing money and that as a result, perhaps their daughter, poor girl, would not marry so well? Or would have to marry an Englishman or a South African? God forbid! Why did poor Philip—who loved Nadia—have to marry that ugly, fat what's-her-name? Because of her enormous dowry? Grandmaman was interested in all this gossip and was often asked to help find a husband or wife for one of her friends. She was very good at matchmaking and helped many of her friends' children to marry well. When it came to her own family, however, Grandmaman did not fare so well.

My cousin Henri died of leukemia three months after his wedding, leaving a young widow who accused the family of hiding the fact that Henri had been sick before he married her.

No one knew how to deal with her. She would roam the house aimlessly until my grandparents decided to set her up in Alexandria, where she later married again. Another of my cousins, Zaki, fainted on his wedding night. His wife, upset by the rumors that had been circulating about her husband, began to overeat, which strained an already difficult union. I was too young then to understand the rumors, but I later discovered (on my own wedding day!) that Zaki was a homosexual, which in the forties in Cairo was scandalous.

My uncle Albert's son Vita was another marriage statistic. Vita had gone to medical school and had graduated as a gynecologist. His father, however, lost his fortune in a disastrous business venture and could not help his son to establish an office. The only solution left to him was to find a rich woman to marry. The whole family was put to task to find him a wife. Tante Odette came up with a candidate, an English army ambulance driver whom she had met at a party at the Sporting Club. Odette reported breathlessly that although the girl was away on duty in the desert, our family could meet her parents, who happened to be visiting Cairo for the weekend. A dinner was planned. Grandmaman, to Ahmet's delight, ordered a French repast. Mr. and Mrs. Anderson were very English: he was tall and wiry, with a rather wan face and a pencil-thin mustache; his wife was strikingly patrician. My cousin Vita was pleased—imagining the daughter's resemblance to her mother—as were his parents. A few days later their daughter showed up, and disaster struck. Mary was tall, but she was also fat and plain, a bad copy of her father. Vita was devastated and wanted to drop the whole idea. I was twelve at the time, and I felt particularly mature as I sat beside him on the garden bench as he smoked a cigar moaning, *"Elle est affreuse . . . je ne peux pas l'épouser! Mais je dois . . ."* ("She is horrid . . . I cannot marry her! But I must . . ."). When I responded that I would never marry someone whom I did not like, he tried to explain to me that his parents had lost a lot of money because of the war and that it was his responsibility to take care of them. The wedding took place in Alexandria, and Grandmaman, who adored Vita, refused to go.

Vita's fiancée and I did not get along. I was probably quite rude to her because of what Vita had said to me. So when the wedding was arranged, she refused to have me as a bridesmaid, which I half expected. My cousin Renée was chosen instead.

The couple set up house in Alexandria, but to Vita's frustration and anger, the dowry was never paid, so his sacrifice had been in vain. After the war, they left for England, and a few months later he divorced her. I never saw him again, but I often think of him and wonder what would have happened if he had listened to his twelve-year-old cousin.

The top floor of the house was occupied by Tante Lydia, my grandmother's oldest daughter, with her husband and their five children. My cousin Meg was number three. A romantic loner, Meg went on endless walks by herself (shocking all of us) and read poetry in the garden, refusing invitations for merrymaking with her friends. She was studious and bright, but by her senior year in high school she was having serious difficulties with mathematics. Tante Lydia decided that Meg needed a private tutor, and the head of the math department of the French *lycée* was hired to help her. Pierre was French, in his late thirties and very pleasant. He came twice a week to our house to teach Meg calculus. All the children liked him, and when I, who was terrible in math, needed help, Pierre was always willing to assist. At the end of the year, after passing her exams with flying colors, Meg announced that she was marrying Pierre. This was the first time that a young girl just out of high school chose a husband without the family's help. It set a precedent later followed by other cousins.

Everyone in the family—led this time by Tante Lydia—immediately set out to dissuade her. Who was Pierre? What future could a math teacher in a French *lycée* have? He would want to go back to France after the war, and then what? He was too old...she was only seventeen! There were endless family councils; screams and fights were heard throughout the house. But in the end Tante Lydia gave in, and a date for the nuptials was set. The wedding, like most Jewish weddings of that period, was held in the apartment of the bride; weddings were rarely held in a synagogue. Meg's wedding was held in her parent's third-floor apartment, and I was both bridesmaid and flower girl, a seven-year-old dressed simply in a short, silky white dress with a ribbon in my hair. Only the immediate family attended the wedding, which was joyless despite the fact that Meg was happy and radiant. It turned out that hers was the only marriage of Tante Lydia's children that lasted—for thirty years, in fact. After the war they went to live in Paris. Pierre died in 1975, and Meg is still alive but quite old.

Grandmaman had had nine children, and by the time we arrived in Egypt, all but the two youngest daughters, Marise and Monique, were married. The "problem" was Marise. She was, as my grandmother would sometimes whisper, "slow," a euphemism for mentally retarded. Marise was beautiful: tall, slim, blond, with enormous blue eyes that always had a faraway look. As a young girl Marise had been kept home and had learned how to read and write with a private tutor. I loved Marise because she remained a little girl in spirit, if not in body, and genuinely enjoyed playing games with me. If we went for a walk, Grandmaman would always say, "Hold her hand tightly! Don't lose her." Marise loved flowers and had an unusual gift for painting. She would sit for hours on the terrace in front of an easel and paint the blooms she saw in the garden below. She often offered her charming watercolors to me, which I proudly displayed all over the walls of my bedroom. I took them along with me when I left Egypt after the war. Only a few years ago was I obliged to throw them out since the paper had yellowed and crumbled. My grandparents were told that Marise should not marry, a piece of advice that they rejected—they had never accepted the fact that their beautiful child was retarded in the first place. If she remained unmarried, people would talk. I also believe that my grandmother was worried about Marise's happiness. Like everyone of her generation, Grandmaman believed marriage was the ultimate—the only—fulfillment.

The family was divided, however. Tante Fortuné, the most modern of my aunts, felt that my grandparents should abide by the doctors' directives and let Marise stay home. Tante Marie believed Marise should leave the house and marry. When the search for a suitable husband began, Tante Marie was put in charge. After a few months and a couple of tries, Tante Marie found a candidate, a low-level employee in my grandfather's department store. Promised a high position in the store, Abel agreed to marry Marise. A small wedding, just for the immediate family, was planned and I, at age eight, was the sole bridesmaid. I can still remember my dress: a long, puffy, white tulle dress with small pink flowers around the neckline. Naturally I thought I looked like an angel and wanted to wear it every day. Marise was dressed in a flowing white silk gown with blue and white flowers in her blond hair. She looked beautiful, but the look on her face was even more absent than usual; she did not seem to know exactly what was happening to her. The religious ceremony took place in our living room. I walked in front of her with a basket of pink rose petals that I was directed to scatter onto the carpet, but in my concern for Marise, I forgot to do so. During the ceremony I stood next to her while she held my hand tightly. The whole event was upsetting to me. My cousin Renée had told me that she had heard that Abel was unpleasant and rough. A small dinner followed the wedding. I cannot even remember what we ate or how it was served. I cried in a corner, realizing that I was losing a friend.

The next day, Marise came into my room, sat on my bed, and cried. I had no clear idea why, but we held on to one another tightly for several minutes. Years later, Aishe told me that Marise's wedding night had frightened her. Nine months later Marise gave birth to a little girl who did not survive, and Marise herself died a few weeks later from an aneurysm. Her husband, to the family's obvious relief, disappeared from our lives. For weeks I moped through the house, unhappy, having once again lost someone I really loved. I think, too, that I must have felt I let Marise down, that I should have protected her from her husband. I was also very angry with my grandparents, not understanding their decision to marry Marise to Abel, and for a couple of weeks I would not talk to them. One afternoon, in a fit of rage, I took a pair of scissors to my beloved bridesmaid's dress, cutting it into small pieces. My grandmother found me on the floor surrounded by a small hill of tattered tulle. She took me in her arms, and we both cried. "You were right," she whispered in my ear. I loved her then more than ever.

My aunt Monique, the baby of the family, was the exact opposite of Marise. Small, thin, and with a mass of curly auburn hair like my grandmother, Monique was independent, stubborn, and very bright. To the horror of my entire family, Monique announced on her eighteenth birthday that she wanted to attend the university and—unthinkable—work in an office. Palacci women were supposed to marry, take care of their appearance, go to the Sporting Club, swim, play tennis, meet their friends, and at night appear on the roof of the Semiramis Hotel (the best in town) to dance the night away. There were arguments every night and again, Tante Fortuné came to Monique's rescue: "Why not the university?" she convinced my grandmother. "She would make an even more attractive wife, would she not? She'll certainly marry before she even finds a job!"

Every morning Monique was driven to Cairo University while we were dropped off at the French *lycée.* The following fall, Monique announced that she had a part-time job at the English Officer's Club as a secretary to the director. My grandfather was incensed, but oddly, my grandmother took Monique's side, claiming that she'd meet eligible men. Tante Marie shook her head, while my cousins Alice and Renée, who were about to finish school, regarded Monique with envy.

For the next few months we saw very little of Monique. Her life seemed to me very mysterious. She would go to the university in the morning, then directly to the club, where she would spend the evening at least three times a week. My grandfather complained all the while that she was not home enough and always added, "Why on earth must you work?" Monique would laugh and then kiss my grandfather on the forehead, telling him he was from the old school but that she loved him.

Two months later, in the early evening when the whole family was sitting on the terrace eating *mezze*—the small dishes of different appetizers served most evenings—and gossiping, Monique burst in and dropped a bomb at my family's feet. "My fiancé is outside and I'm bringing him in. Please be nice . . . and, Papa . . . no questions yet." Two minutes later Monique came back, dragging a shy, reluctant young man. George Harris was an English officer of medium height, about thirty, with a receding hairline and a slight paunch. Introductions were made while Alice and Renée giggled. George sat down between my grandparents, looking quite miserable. Grandmaman was smiling, Grandpère peering down sternly, and all my aunts and cousins were brazenly ogling "poor George," as he would be referred to by the younger generation from then on.

The next days were full of the usual bickering about the dowry; my grandfather also made discreet inquiries about his future son-in-law. To my grandparent's dismay, Monique and George announced that after the wedding they planned to emigrate to Kenya, where Tante Marie's children had a ranch. Yet another couple deserting home! I was going to be once more a bridesmaid. Since Marise's death, the idea of being a bridesmaid had lost all its glamour, but this time I was not to be the only one: Monique had selected two of my cousins to be part of the *cortège*. George's credentials were honorable, however, and their wedding remains in my memory as a typically exuberant and elaborate affair.

The ceremony was to be held under a tent in the garden behind the house. George was Protestant, so there would be no authentic Judaic rituals, but the rabbi had agreed to officiate. This was not unusual, as intermarriage was frequent during the war. There would be a cocktail reception in the garden with Champagne and petits fours (the Swiss pastry shop and *salon de thé*, Groppi's, would, of course, make the petits fours and their famous three-tiered wedding cake), followed by a buffet dinner cooked by Ahmet and supplemented by specialties prepared by my competitive aunts. Extra servants would be hired, and there would be an Arab singer and her *tackti* (orchestra). For weeks before the big day, the household resounded with gossipy phone calls, furious cleaning, and dressmakers scurrying around all the women. Except, of course, Monique. She would be called for fittings but was nowhere to be found. Poor George was overwhelmed by the family's exuberance and wanted to avoid them at any cost. Monique was already trying to make George happy by following him on his "excursions."

A few days before the wedding, the large tent with embroidered panels was erected in the garden. A red carpet was rolled from the front gate to the main entrance of the house; another established a path to the tent. Living and dining room doors were flung open, and several large tables were set lavishly. I wasn't allowed anywhere in the house except my bedroom and—to my delight—the kitchen. Ahmet was a whirling dervish, barking orders to the five helpers in the kitchen, working feverishly. Even I was employed to shell peas (I popped one in my mouth for every ten I shelled and got sick later that night), peel garlic, and help Aishe roll the vine leaves.

On the day of the wedding, Grandmaman, nervous but beautiful in her beige lace dress and long strings of pearls hanging richly over her opulent chest, appeared to me like a queen. Monique, her curly hair crowned with a small pearl cap and a long veil, stood smiling in the mirror while the dressmaker, with pins in her mouth, made some last-minute adjustments to her dress. At five o'clock the guests arrived and were greeted by ushers who led them to the tent, where George, splendid in his army uniform, stood nervously next to his captain. The guests and the rest of our family were waiting for the bride. Alice, Renée, and I—bridesmaids—were fussing in the hall, admiring our white silk dresses and the artfully arranged flowers in our hair. I carried a very tall candle, and Alice and Renée held bouquets of white and pink flowers.

I don't remember much about the ceremony, being preoccupied by the candle that threatened to spill wax on my angelic dress. When I heard *"mabrouk!"* ("Congratulations!") uttered many times, I knew that the ceremony was over. As each guest left the tent, everyone was given a small silver ashtray filled with white- and silver-coated almonds wrapped in white tulle and tied with a pink ribbon. I still have my collection of silver ashtrays, culled from the many weddings I attended as a bridesmaid. After the ceremony, guests listened to the Arabic singer, eating petits fours and drinking Champagne until the dinner gong sounded. I had not been allowed in the dining room before the wedding, so I was overwhelmed by the amount of food displayed on a long table, behind which stood four waiters in rich *galabeyyas* with broad red sashes. On one table were the little dishes, the *mezze:* vine leaves stuffed with saffron rice, tomatoes, parsley and onion; eggplant purée mixed with yogurt with tiny meatballs floating in it; fried eggplant with garlic; eggplant caviar; lamb's brain salad prepared with scallions, garlic, lemon, and cumin; fried ground chicken balls; and artichoke hearts stewed in olive oil. Thin slices of *batarekh* (pressed smoked fish roe) were set on toast rounds and topped with crème fraîche and lemon zest. There were fried mussels, slices of French *pâté;*

FRIED MUSSELS

TO MAKE A BATTER, dissolve 1 package dried yeast and 1 teaspoon sugar in 1 cup water. Set aside for 15 minutes to proof.

MIX 1 CUP FLOUR, 2 tablespoons melted butter, $\frac{1}{4}$ teaspoon salt, and 2 egg yolks in a bowl. Add the yeast, mix well, and keep covered in a warm place for 10 minutes. Beat 2 egg whites until stiff and fold into the flour mixture. The batter will be fairly liquid.

SCRUB 3 PINTS of fresh mussels and place in a large saucepan with $\frac{1}{2}$ cup white wine and salt and pepper. Cover and cook over high heat, shaking the pan occasionally, for 7 to 10 minutes, or until all the shells open. Remove the mussels from the shells. Reserve the juice for making the *Tarator* sauce.

DUST THE MUSSELS with flour, then dip into the batter and fry in 2 cups hot oil until golden brown. Serve hot or cold with *Tarator* sauce. It will serve 4.

baskets of thinly sliced Italian salami; *loubiya,* a salad of black-eyed peas, one of my favorite dishes; and a celeriac and fennel salad in lemony vinaigrette. Ahmet had slaved the entire night before the wedding making hundreds of tiny hot *sambousaks.*

A second table held meats, fish, and vegetables. I stared at huge roast legs of lamb; Ahmet's famous duck ballottine; tiny squabs stuffed with rice and roasted almonds (a famous dish made especially for young couples to wish them a sweet life full of love); *kofta,* small meatballs in an apricot sauce; and countless other delicacies. Dessert included not only the wedding cake but ice cream made from buffalo milk, pyramids of apricot pudding, and Middle Eastern pastries such as *kunafa*, stuffed with pistachios; *zalabia*, tiny, light, crisp deep-fried dough soaked in honey and orange blossoms; and paper-thin filo stuffed with chopped walnuts. I ate until I could no longer move, while I listened to the wailing tones of the singer. Around ten o'clock, Monique and George left for Mena House, the hotel facing the Pyramids, where all couples spent the first few days of their honeymoon. Poor George, who would remain forever frightened of my grandfather, was happy to escape our overwhelming family. Theirs would prove to be a happy marriage although they had no children, which saddened Monique. After the war, they left for South Africa. Monique kept in touch with me while I lived in Paris, but once I moved to New York, I lost track of her. The one bit of news I heard was that George had died in the late 1970s.

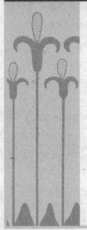

TARATOR SAUCE

This sauce was served with hot or cold fish at weddings and parties.

REMOVE THE CRUSTS from 2 slices of white bread. Soak the bread in some water, then squeeze it dry. Place in a food processor with 1 cup pine nuts, 2 chopped garlic cloves, and the juice of 2 lemons. Process until all the ingredients are puréed. If the sauce is too thick, add some of the juice reserved from making the mussels (or fish stock) and process until smooth. This makes about 2 cups.

Bridesmaids were given a gift of gold by the bride—a tradition in our family, and just before leaving, Monique handed the three of us a gold bangle. These bangles came in handy years later, when my husband and I lived in Italy and were broke. I would sell one of my bangles, which would take care of us for the next two weeks. Of the twenty or so I had, two remain, and I wear them always. One was my grandfather's present to me when I left for Paris (I would never see him again). The other was Monique's gift to me on her wedding day. Today, when I look at my oldest daughter, I am reminded of Monique. Marianne is stubborn and bright and always says when she makes a decision that is unpopular, "Don't worry, I know what I'm doing."

I realize as I write about these weddings that the thread that held my family together in Egypt is now broken forever.

LOUBIYA

A salad of black-eyed peas.

SOAK 1 POUND of black-eyed peas in water to cover overnight. Drain the peas and place in a saucepan, cover with water, and bring to a boil. Reduce the heat and simmer for 40 minutes, or until tender. Drain and set aside to cool.

PLACE 7 GARLIC CLOVES in a mortar, sprinkle with salt, and pound until you make a paste. Gradually work in 2 tablespoons lemon juice and 2 to 3 tablespoons olive oil. Add salt and pepper and pour over the peas. Toss and sprinkle with 1 tablespoon chopped parsley. This will serve 4 or more.

KOFTA [MEATBALLS WITH APRICOT SAUCE]

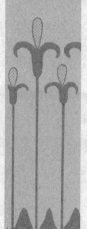

MIX I POUND GROUND LAMB with 2 small leeks that have been washed well and finely chopped, I tablespoon raw rice, and 2 eggs. Mix in I tablespoon olive oil, I tablespoon chopped fresh cilantro, and salt and pepper. Form balls the size of walnuts. Place the meatballs in a large saucepan with I 1/2 cups chicken stock. Simmer for 20 minutes, adding water if necessary. Drain the meatballs and cool.

ROLL THE MEATBALLS in flour and melt 2 tablespoons butter in a large skillet. When the butter is hot, add the meatballs and sauté for 5 to 6 minutes, until nicely browned.

FOR THE SAUCE, soak I cup dried apricots in water to cover for 2 hours. Drain the apricots and place in a food processor and purée. Add 10 chopped garlic cloves, I teaspoon ground coriander, and I tablespoon olive oil. Purée. Then, with the motor running, slowly add 3 cups chicken stock. Add salt and pepper to taste, transfer to a saucepan, and simmer, stirring with a wooden spoon, for 5 minutes. Pour the sauce on the meatballs and serve. This makes 4 servings.

Although I have tried in vain to keep my own children close to me, they have left our big house just as I did when I married and emigrated to America. Two of them have started their own families far away, and I know now what my grandparents must have felt upon the dissolution of their little dynasty.

CHAPTER 5

Grandmaman's Poker Day

MY GRANDMOTHER HAD MANY FRIENDS AND RELATIVES.
Among her friends and family members were
eight women who had known each other since
they were children. A few, like Tante Marie,
were widows with children; others had husbands who worked for my grandfather or
were old friends of his. The eight spent hours
on the telephone every day, exchanging
gossip, talking about their children, or complaining about their servants, cooks, or
daughters- and sons-in-law. Each woman had
son jour de recevoir, her day to receive guests in

the afternoon for a game of poker or canasta. Later, in early evening, their husbands would join them for dinner; after dinner, the women and the men would play high-stake games of poker until the wee hours of the morning. Hundreds and sometimes thousands of Egyptian pounds would pass hands, all in good fun.

I hated these days, since my life would be turned upside down. Grandmaman's day was Saturday, every eight weeks. Preparations started the day before. Early in the morning, before the sun got too hot, the whole household would be put to work cleaning the house, washing the terrace, and cooking a feast.

First the windows of the living room were flung wide open. Then the oriental rugs were picked up and tossed over the veranda railing. Abdullah would whip the dust off the rug with great energy, using a reed beater shaped like a four-leaf clover at the end of a long stick. While he beat, he sang a song. I would hear him and immediately appear in my night-gown and beg Abdullah to let me try. Within five minutes I would be covered with dust from head to toe. Suddenly my grandmother would appear, screaming at Abdullah that he had absolutely no brains allowing me do something so unla-dylike. She would grab me by the arm and banish me back to my rooms, ordering Aishe to give me a good scrubbing in the bathtub.

Afterward, the rugs would be put back in place, the furni-ture would be dusted, and four or five card tables would be set in the middle of the living room. Great quantities of flow-ers would arrive, and Marise, who was considered the artist of the family, would arrange them around the room. No one was allowed in the salon for the next twenty-four hours.

For poker day, the "good" silver, the most ornate and heavy cutlery, came out of the drawers, and the silver coffee service, which every Egyptian family seemed to have sitting on a silver tray on a sideboard, would be polished. Aishe and the porter's wife would be given the task of polishing the silver. I would sit with them, listening to their gossip about the men servants of the adjoining houses. Between polishing and gossiping they would munch on dried melon seeds, placing them between their front teeth and cracking them open. I learned very quickly how to do it, a habit to which my grandmother strongly objected. When they were afraid to eat the seeds because she was too near, they chewed on *mastic,* a sort of resin, transparent and hard as a stone, which would, after heroic chewing, turn into a sticky white paste. When I was six, Aishe tried to teach me how to chew, but my baby teeth hurt so much that I quickly abandoned the idea, to the great relief of my grandmother, who loved to say about those who chewed, *"Ils ressemblent à des vaches espagnoles"* ("They look like Spanish cows"). I still don't chew gum and often try to stop my own grandchild Matthew from chewing bubble gum and blowing bubbles with it. Matthew thinks I am odd. "You're not an American, Grandmaman," he likes to say with a little smile as he tries to entice me to buy him some bubble gum.

On Fridays before poker days, Grandmaman and Ahmet would go together to the market, not in the open carriage, as when Grandmaman went to market with Abdullah, but in my grandfather's car. Ahmet sat next to the chauffeur, and I— when I was allowed to accompany them—would be in the backseat next to Grandmaman. On our return, my seat would be filled with packages, and I would be squeezed in front between the chauffeur and Ahmet.

The scene at the market was quite different when Ahmet was with us. My grandmother was more subdued and would stand quietly to the side while Ahmet argued with the vendors about prices and quality of the food. However, one day a shattering event occurred; it might easily have destroyed my grandmother's favorite pastime had not Ahmet saved the day. We were standing between the poultry vendor and the watermelon vendor when suddenly Ahmet started to scream at a young man next to us, accusing him of stealing his money. A fight ensued, and suddenly it grew ugly. The crowd that gathered seemed hostile, and the man turned his attention to my grandmother and began hurling insults at her. I will never forget the fear on Grandmaman's face. She took me in her arms, enveloping me as if to protect me, nearly choking me while Ahmet and the watermelon man tried to calm the young man and the crowd. The police arrived, searched the young man, found Ahmet's wallet on him, and arrested him. They then escorted us back to the car. This was the only time I was allowed to sit in the back. My grandmother held me tightly, and I could feel her body still trembling from the fear that that incident had provoked. That night my grandfather scolded my grandmother and Ahmet and forbade Grandmaman ever to go shopping at the market again. For the next two months Grandmaman sent Ahmet to shop alone, but she missed the adventure of going to the market and soon resumed her weekly trips. I, however, had to wait a full year before I was allowed to accompany her.

With the poker-day cleaning and marketing done, the kitchen would be thrown into turmoil. Grandmaman herself would prepare her famous *sambusacks,* large eggplants would be charing on the primus, several legs of lamb would be marinating on the counter, and on a small table Aishe and the chauffeur would be stuffing grape leaves with a mixture of rice and chopped lamb. If I sat quietly near Aishe, I was

STUFFED GRAPE LEAVES

WASH A 1-POUND JAR OF VINE LEAVES under cold running water to rinse off the brine. Place in a bowl, cover with boiling water, and let stand for 5 minutes. Drain and cool.

MIX 1 POUND OF CHOPPED LAMB with 1 cup raw rice, ½ cup chopped parsley, ⅓ cup olive oil, ¼ cup lemon juice, 1 tablespoon cumin, and salt and pepper to taste. Mix well. Spread out the leaves. In the center of a vine leaf place 1 tablespoon of the meat-rice stuffing. Fold the base of the leaf up and over the stuffing, fold in the sides, and roll the leaf tightly to make a cylinder about 2½ inches long and ½ to ¾ inch thick. Continue until you have used all the stuffing.

COVER THE BOTTOM of a heavy saucepan with loose vine leaves. Place a layer of stuffed vine leaves, close together and seam side down, along the bottom. Arrange another tightly packed layer on top of that, continuing until all the stuffed leaves have been added. Cover with 3 or 4 loose vine leaves. Pour in ¼ cup olive oil and 2 cups chicken broth. Cover and bring to a boil. Lower the heat and simmer for 45 minutes. When cooked, arrange the stuffed leaves on a platter and pour ¼ cup lemon juice over them. Serve hot or cold with yogurt or tehina. This makes about 30 to 40 vine leaves.

allowed to stay in the kitchen and help roll the grape leaves. Meanwhile Ahmet would be preparing a ballottine of duck to be served sliced with a dark, smooth jelly. I loved to watch as Ahmet deftly cut the duck's back so it lay flat on the kitchen marble, then slowly and carefully deboned it. He would remove the duck meat, mince it with spices, and add pistachio nuts. The duck skin would then be rolled around the stuffing, and Ahmet with a needle and thread would sew it shut, making it look like a fat sausage. The scent of the roasting duck would permeate the house and make me very hungry. After a while, I would forget myself and begin chatting away, asking questions or begging a taste of something, often stealing some pistachios that Ahmet painstakingly had shelled that morning. Ahmet, in an unusual fit of exasperation, would then throw me out of the kitchen, and I would roam the house like a lost soul. I felt once more abandoned, for it seemed to me that I was nowhere welcomed.

My aunts prepared desserts. Tante Fortuné made her special dish of prunes stuffed with walnuts in a brandy syrup; Tante Lydia made a sort of multicolor tower of Jell-O that would invariably fall after the first person helped himself. It would look a mess, but Grandmaman never said anything because, as she explained to me one day, Lydia did not know how to cook. Tante Becca would bring a dish of her light, crisp, and golden *zalabia*, which I would gobble down if no one was looking.

Saturday morning, the remaining dishes were prepared. For the *mezze*, small pieces of lamb's liver were fried with onions and cumin; they would be sprinkled with lemon juice and minced parsley and served cold. *Hummus*, the traditional chickpea dish, was decorated with slivered almonds. There

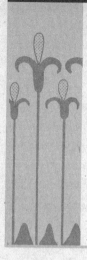

APRICOT PUDDING

PLACE ½ POUND DRIED APRICOTS in a bowl. Cover with warm water and allow to soak overnight. Drain. Place the apricots, 4 large eggs, ¼ cup heavy cream, I tablespoon rum, and ½ cup sugar in a food processor. Process until the apricots are puréed. Butter a I-quart mold. Pour the apricot purée into the mold. Place the mold in a larger pan filled with hot water and bake in a preheated 350-degree oven for 45 minutes, or until the point of a knife inserted in the middle comes out clean. Cool and unmold on a round platter. Garnish with mint leaves. This will serve 4.

were also tiny artichoke hearts marinated in olive oil, fried ground chicken balls, and, in season, cold tender broad beans. Grandmaman's contribution to the *mezze* were "mimosa eggs," hard-boiled eggs stuffed with egg yolks mashed with mayonnaise and herbs, which I hated but which were very popular with the ladies. There were always thin slices of *batarekh*—salted dried roe of the gray mullet preserved in a sort of waxy skin—on thin toasts. Olives, black or green, would fill silver bowls, as would cucumber pickles. These dishes were served on the terrace while the table in the dining room was made ready for the dinner. Limoges dishes were brought out under the eyes of Grandmaman, who would repeat endlessly to everyone, "Be careful, be careful! These are my best dishes!"

On this day the jewels came out, heavy diamond-studded bracelets, arms full of gold bangles (by the age of ten, I had already ten of them), sparkling diamond rings. Grandmaman did not approve of diamonds and never wore hers. She would say of women covered in diamonds, "They look as if they are wearing a crystal chandelier!" I remember years later, when one of my uncles was trying to marry me off, he would always point out the quality of the pretenders by telling me how many karats my diamond would weigh.

My grandmother would tell me, just before the guests arrived, to go and get dressed, comb my hair, and, mainly, put some shoes on. Whenever I came back from school or was at home on weekends, I walked around the house barefoot or I wore *shib-shib,* the flat slippers that Aishe bought for me at the market. They made a flapping noise whenever I walked.

Sometimes a new person would be introduced to the group, and I would be proudly paraded in front of them. "My granddaughter," my grandmother would say to that day's new addition; "She is half French, you know," as if that qualification would add a new dimension to who I was. Then the whispers would start that always upset me: "She is an orphan, you know ... Really? No, I did not know. ... Well, not quite, her mother ... you know ... Alexandria ... Beirut ... left the child here with Marguerite ..." And it would go on for several minutes. The women would look at me with pity, which I resented terribly, especially when my aunt Lydia would ask her younger daughter, Renée, who was just a year older than me, to come and say hello. Renée, tall, thin and blond, would gracefully make the rounds, and I would be forgotten as the women exclaimed in their chanting voices, *"Elle est adorable ... comme elle est mignone!"* ("She is adorable ... how pretty she is!").

The food was served twice on that day. When the ladies arrived around four o'clock, they would be served tea with petits fours from Groppi's, the famous Swiss pastry store in

Cairo. Then they would sit around the four tables and begin to play. At each table was a member of the family. Grandmaman was always in a black lace blouse, and her pearls looked regal. She had told me the story of that pearl necklace: that my grandfather had given her a strand of pearls for each of their nine children. It went several times around her neck, and while waiting her turn she would often play with the pearls, as if making a signal to her canasta partner. "The pearls will be yours, Colette," she always said, "when you grow up and act like a real lady." Like Grandmaman, the others at the card table would also be all dressed up. Tante Fortuné was the one I admired the most. While everyone else was in black, her dresses would be of red silk covered with large blue roses, or of green velvet edged in gold. My grandmother was horrified. For her and her friends, once you got married you wore subdued colors, and by the time you were forty you wore black or gray. But Tante Fortuné would laugh and employ an argument that Grandmaman could never object to: "My husband loves it!" Years later at my own wedding, Tante Fortuné arrived in a black dress with an enormous red bow tied to her hips. The younger generation loved it, and she was the toast of the party.

While the women were playing, Renée and I were often asked to pass around little tea sandwiches, while Abdullah, dressed in his best *galabeyya*, would glide through the tables and ask which the women preferred, tea or coffee. The silver coffee set would be brought in, and European coffee, which was then very fashionable, would be served.

Within half an hour, though, we were forgotten. Renée would go back to her floor, and I would roam around the house, trying to find someone to talk to. Aishe was always too busy helping Ahmet; Ahmet would not allow me in the

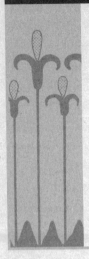

STUFFED ZUCCHINI AND RED PEPPERS

HALVE ABOUT 1 POUND small zucchini and scoop out the centers. Cut the tops off 4 red bell peppers and remove all the seeds.

MIX 1 POUND CHOPPED BEEF with 1 pound chopped veal; add 3 tablespoons pine nuts, salt and pepper to taste, 2 minced garlic cloves, and 2 tablespoons olive oil. Fill the zucchini and the peppers with the meat. Place side by side in a pan. Drizzle with 2 tablespoons olive oil and add 2 cups chicken broth to the pan. Bake in a preheated 375-degree oven for 45 minutes. Serve hot or cold with yogurt. This is enough for 4.

kitchen, and if I returned to the living room, my grandmother would signal me to get out and usually would say, "You are distracting the players!" I would end up in my room, sulking until dinner was announced.

Canasta was played with feverish intensity, and arguments sometimes broke out between partners over foolish melds or discards. Tante Marie's table was the most exciting. Tante Marie was an excellent player and often won the game. In the beginning, when my father and mother had settled in after we first came to Cairo, Tante Marie had tried to teach my mother how to play cards. Years later, when we were in Paris, my mother would tell me how much she hated cards, especially canasta, which she found very boring. Poker had seemed more exciting to her, but she had never learned it. She did try to learn bridge—a very popular game among the younger crowd—but even then, she wasn't very good at it. In defense of my mother, I too never learned how to play cards until years later, when I began to play games with my grandchildren. Julien, my youngest grandson, loves to play cards, and I can see in his eyes the same excitement and twinkle that Tante Marie had when she was winning.

Grandmaman always sat with her three best friends and, while playing, would continue to gossip. The women would finish the game, counting their winnings. My grandmother, who was not as good a player, did not often win.

Between seven and eight o'clock, the men would arrive and retire to the terrace, where Abdullah would serve the *mezze*. The women would join them there. This is when the younger members of the family—those not married—would arrive from the different floors of our house. My cousin Zaki called this moment the marriage-go-round. The unmarried young women of the family would slowly walk from table to table, greeting my grandmother's friends, talking about their projects, or simply smiling. Later it would be the turn of the young unmarried men. The women would look over the young men for their daughters or the young women for their sons, mentally calculating the women's dowries, or the future earnings or fortunes of the men. Alice and Nadia, both in their late teens, would come down, parading among the guests, laughing and gossiping afterward, wondering aloud which one had made the best impression. Years later, Alice married an Englishman and moved to England, and Nadia moved to Italy and married an American who had settled there.

At eight-thirty, as dinner was announced, everyone, including the children, would move to the dining room to help themselves from the buffet while oohing and aahing about Ahmet's delicious cooking.

On the table for dinner would be the ballottine, beautifully decorated with egg white and jelly; roast leg of lamb, thinly sliced and served with a parsley sauce; hot, open meat pies with pine nuts; baked noodles with eggplant; several bowls of vegetable salads; cold fried fish served with *Zemino* sauce made with garlic and anchovies—one of my favorite dishes—and five different types of pickles. I would immediately pounce on the ballottine and the fried fish as my grandmother would shake her head in despair over my lack of manners.

Later, the women and men returned to the living room for serious games of poker, with much higher stakes. The names of the players were placed in a silver dish, then drawn to determine who would play with whom.

ANGEL HAIR WITH NUTS AND RAISINS

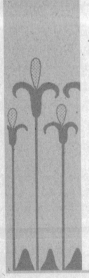

BREAK ½ POUND of angel hair in 3-inch pieces. In a skillet heat 2 tablespoons butter with 1 tablespoon oil. Add 1 onion, thinly sliced; sauté until transparent. Add the angel hair and fry until golden brown. Cover with 3 cups chicken broth, bring to a boil, then lower the heat and simmer until all the broth is absorbed. MEANWHILE ROAST 2 tablespoons slivered almonds and 2 tablespoons chopped hazelnuts in a 350-degree oven until golden. Remove from the oven. In a small skillet heat ½ tablespoon butter. Add 3 tablespoons raisins and sauté until the raisins puff up. Mix the raisins with nuts and add to the pasta. Serve hot with roast chicken. Serves 4.

VEGETABLE SALAD

PEEL, SEED, AND DICE 3 ripe tomatoes and 3 cucumbers. Dice 2 green bell peppers. Peel and chop 2 sweet white onions; chop 1 bunch parsley. Cube 2 red radishes, and peel and mince 2 garlic cloves. Dice 3 celery ribs and quarter 3 Bibb lettuces. Place all the vegetables in a large bowl. In a small bowl mix together 1 tablespoon Dijon mustard, 1 tablespoon red wine vinegar, 3 tablespoons olive oil, and salt and pepper to taste. Pour over the salad and toss. Serves 4.

My grandfather always hoped to have Tante Marie at his table; just before picking up a name, he would make a small sign to my grandmother, trying to figure out which piece of paper bore Tante Marie's name.

Once everyone was sitting down and the card game had really begun, I was sent to bed. In the morning I would slide my hand under my pillow. If I found several pound notes, it meant that Tante Marie had won the night before. This was her gesture toward me, for she understood how lonely and forlorn I was on poker days.

The next morning, life's daily routine would return. The card tables were folded and put away, along with the Limoges china and the best silver. Ahmet would be in good humor, and I was allowed once again to haunt the kitchen when I came back from school, sample what was for dinner, and kick my shoes off.

CHAPTER 6

The Convent

AFTER MY FATHER'S DEATH IN 1939, MY MOTHER traveled. When war was declared in Europe, she had worried about my brother and had tried to have him come back, but her father had convinced her that the war would last only a few months and that my brother would be safe with them. She then decided to leave for Lebanon. My mother loved Beirut, which she used to say reminded her of Paris. She stayed there from 1939 to 1942, calling my grandparents once in a while to see how I was. She never talked to me on the telephone, and she became, as the time went by, some faraway figure that I often fantasized about. In my dreams, she was the perfect mother who one day would come, after which we would all live happily together.

Then one day, I was in the kitchen eating my *goûter* (snack): puréed chickpeas and some triangles of pita that Ahmet had

CHICKPEA PURÉE

COVER 2 CUPS DRIED CHICKPEAS with water and soak overnight. Drain and place in a saucepan with 6 cups water and 2 sliced onions. Bring to a boil, lower the heat, and simmer until tender, about 1 hour. Drain and reserve the water.

PURÉE THE CHICKPEAS in a food processor with $\frac{1}{4}$ cup of the cooking liquid, 5 chopped garlic cloves, and 2 tablespoons fresh lemon juice. Return to the saucepan and simmer for 5 minutes. Season with 2 tablespoons olive oil, 1 teaspoon ground cumin, and salt and pepper.

PLACE 2 TOASTED PITA SQUARES in the bottom of 4 soup plates. Reheat the cooking liquid and spoon some over the bread to soften it. Spoon in the hot chickpea purée and serve.

toasted the way I liked, so crisp that they crumbled as I dipped them. My grandmother sailed into the kitchen followed by my mother—suntanned, young, radiant. My hand, with the piece of pita slathered with *hummus*, froze. I stared rudely until I was interrupted by my grandmother's worried voice. "Say hello to your mother, Colette!" How do you say hello to a mother you

TRADITIONAL HUMMUS

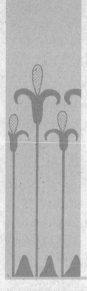

COVER 1 CUP DRIED CHICKPEAS with water and soak overnight. Drain and place in a saucepan with $\frac{1}{2}$ teaspoon salt and water to cover. Bring to a boil, lower the heat, and simmer until tender, about 1 hour. Drain and reserve the water. PLACE THE CHICKPEAS in a food processor with the juice of 2 lemons, 3 minced garlic cloves, and 2 or 3 tablespoons of the cooking liquid. Process until smooth. Add 1 tablespoon olive oil, $\frac{1}{2}$ cup *tehina*, $\frac{1}{2}$ teaspoon ground cumin, and salt and pepper. Process. Transfer to a bowl and sprinkle with 2 tablespoons chopped parsley. Serve with toasted pita. You can substitute one 16-ounce can of chickpeas for the dried. This makes about $1\frac{1}{2}$ cups.

haven't see for three years? I walked slowly toward her. She lunged at me, put her large hands around my face, and exclaimed, "You've grown so much! You're lovely, but you've put on so much weight!... and you're so dark! What happened?" My grandmother cringed. We had just spent a month at the sea, and my copper-colored skin always deepened in tone. Yes, I was rounder than I had been when she left me, but I was far from plump. We left the kitchen and followed my grandmother into the living room in awkward silence. There mother looked at me again, hesitated for a moment, and, after heaving a great, dramatic sigh, began to speak. She told me that she had moved back to Cairo and had taken an apartment in town with an Italian friend whose husband—an engineer—was interned in a prisoner-of-war camp outside of

Alexandria. "The poor woman had nowhere to go. So, you understand, I took her in. We are really the best of friends. And her daughter, Yolande—we call her Lola—is intelligent and very pretty. She'll be your best friend ... you'll see. She can teach you to dress well and act like a lady."

There was another long silence. My grandmother's dressmaker had made the gossamer-thin white cotton dress I was wearing. I liked my dress. I didn't think I was badly dressed. I gave my grandmother a quizzical look, and in a low voice she said that my mother had come to take me home. I would leave that afternoon with her. I started to sob, clinging to Grandmaman. This was not what I had dreamed about all those years. "Colinette," she said, using the pet name she had given me when I had been so upset by my mother's departure. "Don't cry. You will be spending every other weekend here with us." But I continued to weep. Aishe grumbled under her breath while packing my bags, and I suddenly felt defensive. I told her that I was very happy to be leaving, but then when we left, I hugged Aishe very hard and told her that I'd be back every weekend or perhaps more often.

During the war, Cairo had witnessed an influx of Europeans—Jews and non-Jews alike—who sought refuge from the German occupation and the ravages of battle. Peasants from the countryside also flooded the city, looking for jobs. Now downtown was dotted with modern apartment houses with balconies, built to house the wealthier "refugees." My mother's spacious apartment, in one of these new buildings, was on the sixth floor. It had three bedrooms, a dining room, and a living room. Still, it seemed cramped to me compared to my grandparent's mansion. Lola, a petite, blond young woman, about seventeen years old with a cheering smile, greeted me warmly. Her mother, Hélène, on the other hand, I disliked intensely and immediately. Tall, thin, with very black hair and a long, pointed nose, she appeared totally uninterested in me. She and my mother seemed to spend a lot of time huddled together in my mother's room, where I felt I wasn't welcomed. It turned out that I was to share a bedroom with Lola. We dined out that first night in a chic French restaurant, which thrilled me. But later that night, when I crawled into bed, I began to cry again, missing my grandmother, chats on the terrace, and Aishe's whimsical, warm humor.

The next day Lola took me to school, fulfilling the agreement between her mother and mine: babysitting in exchange for room and board. Our mothers went out a lot, so Lola and I were often alone, dining on cold chicken and salad (neither woman knew how to cook). During the week I starved. On the weekends I spent at my grandparents' house, Ahmet and my grandmother stuffed me with my favorite dishes: tender lamb chops, broiled squab, succulent potatoes . . . and of course, *sambousak*. I never talked about my life with my mother, and my grandmother never asked. Life went on this way for several months. One evening in early December, my mother and Hellie (my mother's pet name for Hélène) went out to dinner with their friends, and Lola and I were left alone. The film *Gone with the Wind* was playing in town, and Lola wanted desperately to see it. So as soon as our mothers left, Lola grabbed my hand and we headed for the open-air movie theater. We sat down with a bag of pepitas and glasses of lemonade, waiting for the dark to descend. It was past midnight when we reached home. My mother was waiting for us, furious, screaming at the entire world and especially at me, as if a ten-year-old girl could have coaxed a teenage girl out of going out. The next day, she calmly announced that I would spend Christmas vacation with my grandparents because she was going to Palestine with Hellie to spend the holidays. "Why Palestine?" I didn't understand. My mother then explained that Jesus was born there and for Catholics it was the place to be at Christmas. Catholic? Was I also a Catholic? Why wasn't I going with them? How long was she going to stay? My fears that she would abandon me once again overwhelmed me. "Stop crying!" my mother said. "You are such a baby!"

Christmas was never celebrated at my grandparents' house; indeed, at age ten, I was not even sure exactly what Christmas was. New Year's Eve, however, was fêted on a grand scale with every family member—except, of course, my mother— present. Champagne flowed, French dishes—such as roasted ducks, Ahmet's famous four-meat pâté served with stewed lentils, and my favorite dessert—a rich, moist chocolate mousse served with *eishta*, the thick water buffalo cream—were prepared, and the children received many presents. That year, 1943, my grandfather gave me an adorable, black puppy—a French poodle—whom I named Michette. I also received a bicycle. The next morning, Abdullah taught me how to ride by holding me up and pushing me around the block for hours on end. The bicycle had to stay with my grandparents, but the dog could follow me to my mother's house, as she had uncharacteristically agreed to keep it.

When I went back to my mother's house on January 6, 1943 (I will never forget that date), I was told she had enrolled me at the Convent of the Sacred Heart in Cairo where *"Toutes, Colette, toutes les jeunes filles de bonne famille du Caire sont pensionnaires!"* (boarders). This time, my tantrum was violent: "I hate you you! . . . Take me back to my grandparents!" My mother was unmoved. The next morning, I was driven to the convent, despite my kicks and tears.

The convent was a solid four-story building, built in the early 1900s and set in a very large park in Zamaleck, a residential district across the Nile from my grandparents' house in the Garden City district. It was run by the Mothers of the Sacred Heart, a Parisian missionary order whose school in the rue St. Dominique in Paris was very well known to French Catholics. The convent had two orders of nuns: The Mothers wore an elegant, elaborately folded white bonnet, a black veil, and a black habit. A large silver cross hung heavily over their chests. Both Egyptian and French, all from upper-middle-class backgrounds and rather well educated, the Mothers were responsible for instruction. The poorer nuns—mostly Egyptian—did the housework, cooked, and ran the office. These nuns were called Sisters.

Mère Marin, the Mother Superior, greeted us. We sat in a large living room furnished with gilded armchairs and couches upholstered in red velvet. Vases full of flowers seemed to be everywhere. Paintings depicting the French countryside and an enormous portrait of the founding nun adorned the walls. I was confused. This did not resemble any of the schools I had attended. I was sitting on the edge of my chair pouting, still angry with my mother, when suddenly Mère Marin turned to me and said sweetly, "And what is our little pagan interested in?" Pagan? I wasn't sure I knew what the word meant. But why was she calling me that? My mother smiled and said that my being a pagan was not for long and that she hoped that I would start my lessons very soon. What lessons? I thought I caught both women exchanging a conspiratorial glance. I longed to be back at my grandparents' house, doing

CHRISTMAS FOUR-MEAT PATE

SEASON 1½ POUNDS CHOPPED VEAL with
1 teaspoon minced garlic, 1 tablespoon tarragon,
3 tablespoons cognac, 1 egg, and salt and pepper.
Mix and set aside.

CUT 1½ POUNDS LEAN PORK into ½-inch
strips. Season with salt, pepper, and ½ tablespoon
chopped fresh sage. Mix well and set aside.

REMOVE THE CASINGS from 1½ pounds
sweet Italian sausage. Season the meat with ½
teaspoon minced garlic, 2 tablespoons chopped
fresh parsley, and 3 tablespoons cognac. Mix well
and set aside.

HEAT 1 TABLESPOON olive oil in a skillet. Add
6 trimmed chicken livers and sauté for 2 minutes.
Carefully add 2 tablespoons cognac and ignite.
When the flames die down, remove from the heat
and season with salt and pepper. Set aside.

CUT 2 BONELESS and skinless chicken breasts
into ½-inch strips and set aside.

LINE A 1½-QUART TERRINE with ½ pound
thinly sliced pork fat, reserving any excess. Spoon
in half the sausage meat and cover with the strips
of chicken breast. Spoon in half the veal, and
cover with strips of pork fat and the lean pork.

PLACE THE CHICKEN LIVERS in a row down
the center of the terrine and line on both sides
with ½ cup pimiento-stuffed green olives. Cover
the livers with the remaining veal and top the
veal with the remaining sausage.

PLACE A BAY LEAF on the center of the pâté.
Seal tightly with aluminum foil. Set the terrine in

[CONTINUED]

a larger pan with hot water and bake in a preheated 375-degree oven for $1\frac{1}{2}$ hours.
REMOVE FROM THE OVEN and weight the top
with several cans placed on the foil. When
cooled, refrigerate, still weighed, overnight.
TO SERVE, turn the pâté out from the terrine
and slice very thin. Serve with toast.

my homework, running up and down the stairs, peeping into
each kitchen to see what was for dinner. But for the next four
years, the convent would be my home during the week.

I said a cold goodbye to my mother, refusing to kiss her.
She added as she was leaving that my grandfather's chauffeur
would pick me up on Friday so I might spend the following
weekend with them. A nun led me down a gloomy corridor
and up two flights to a dormitory filled with surprising sunlight from its broad windows. There were twelve beds, each
surrounded with a white, hospital-like curtain. The nun, Mère
Larvulla, pointed to a bed near a window and said that it was
mine. Next to the bed was a small night table. "Put your personal things in here," she said, "and then I'll show you your
closet. You will unpack later when Mohamed brings up your
suitcase." Mère Larvulla's face was severe, and I knew, as only
children know, that she and I would not get along. She looked
too much like Tante Marie. I also called her "the cockroach"
(my nickname for Tante Marie) when I complained about her
to my friends. She always found me wanting. I would
announce to my friends at least once a week, "The cockroach
has punished me. I am sure God will punish her also!"

Later, I was introduced to another pinched and stern nun who, I was told, was the mistress of studies. Mère Baiocchi was tall and wore round metal glasses. She took me to my classroom; I was entering the eighth grade. As the door opened, fifteen heads turned to look at me. Each girl wore an identical uniform: a below-the-knee pleated blue skirt, a white cotton blouse with a round collar tied with blue pompoms. (You had to make your own pompoms, I learned. For a long time I tried to convince the nuns that we could make different-color pompoms, but to no avail. Years later, I taught my own daughters, then my grandchildren, how to make them.) As I sat down in my first class, a few of the girls smiled warmly... or were they smirking? I couldn't tell.

Our day started very early in the morning. The nuns woke us with a bell at six o'clock. It was always cold in the morning, and there was never enough hot water. The older girls got to the bathroom first, then the younger ones. I used to put my clothes under my mattress in the evening so that my underwear would be warm the next day. We dressed quickly, and then went down to the chapel, where we would hear Mass. The Muslim girls, daughters of rich Egyptians, who attended because of the school's high academic standards, were allowed to sleep until seven-thirty. After Mass, we went to a breakfast of *café au lait* with buttered bread and jam. Once a month we stood in line for a teaspoon of cod liver oil; needless to say, we all hated this. Then we went to class. I went to catechism class every morning. I had been told by Mère Marin that I was born to become a Catholic like my mother, but first I had to learn about what little Jesus had done for me. I wasn't interested, I said; I wanted to stay what I was, although I did not quite know what I meant by that since my grandparents and

I had never talked about being Jewish. But I knew I could sleep late like the Muslim girls. Mère Marin explained patiently that my mother had requested my baptism in early February so that I could have my first Communion in March 1944 with all the other girls of my age. I finally agreed because I wanted to please my mother.

I remember well all the girls in my class: Aimée Habra, whose father was an important civil servant; Marie-Thérèse Franceschi, an Italian whose father was interned in a camp; Christiane Crepi, a French girl whose father was fighting with the English army; and Colette Pascal, whose father was an engineer with the Suez Canal and rarely went home on weekends. She was to become my best friend.

Lunch—drab and weakly seasoned for the most part—was served at twelve-thirty. I sorely missed the *ful* sandwiches that Ahmet used to sneak to me. After lunch we would have classes for two more hours. We were then sent into the park to play near a grotto with a statue of Our Lady of Lourdes, to whom the convent was dedicated. Dinner was at seven o'clock, and not much tastier than lunch. During the meal, we had to remain silent while a nun read to us from the life of the saint whose birthday fell on that day. I had not known before this that Colette was a saint whose life had been quite exciting. She had been very independent and had left her father's house at the age of sixteen to follow her lover. Abandoned soon afterward, she begged in the streets, then repented of all her sins and went into a convent to become a nun.

Naturally I discovered the convent kitchen and Soeur Leila, the cook. She became my "Ahmet," and whenever I had free time, or was given a choice of chores to do as a punishment, I'd run to the kitchen to help out. Although Soeur Leila was a fine

cook, she was restricted by the administrators, who spent next
to nothing on food. They also insisted on bland dishes. But she
excelled on Fridays, when she prepared lentils in lieu of meat
or fish. My grandmother had taught me to eat lentils and lentil
sprouts when I was five. She'd line a dish with moist cotton,
scatter lentils over it, and place it by the window. Two days later,
white threads would appear; a day after that, tiny leaves. I was
enchanted, and soon afterward every flat surface of my room
held a saucer of burgeoning seeds. We always ate lentil sprouts
on New Year's Day as a sign of a new beginning. Also, Ahmet
used to make a dish I loved: red lentils, redolent of cumin and
garlic and sprinkled with cilantro. Soeur Leila made an excellent

SOEUR LEILA'S RED LENTIL STEW

PLACE 2 CUPS SPLIT RED LENTILS in a
saucepan with 4 cups water, I large peeled onion,
I large quartered tomato, I carrot, and 2 small
zucchini, each cut into I-inch pieces. Bring to a
boil, lower the heat, cover, and simmer for about
20 minutes, stirring occasionally. Purée the
entire mixture in a food processor and return
to the saucepan. Stir in I teaspoon ground
cumin, ⅓ pound vermicelli or angel hair broken
into small pieces, and salt and pepper. Simmer
for 10 minutes.

CHOP I LARGE ONION and sauté until golden
in 2 tablespoons olive oil. Add to the lentils and
simmer for 5 minutes. Sprinkle with 2 tablespoons chopped fresh parsley and serve with
croutons made from pita. This will serve 4.

LENTIL SOUP

PEEL A LARGE ONION, stick it with a whole clove, and place it in a saucepan with 1 pound lentils, 1 bay leaf, 8 cups chicken stock, and salt and pepper. Bring to a boil over high heat, then reduce the heat and simmer, skimming occasionally, until the lentils are tender, about 30 minutes. Discard the onion and bay leaf and stir in 2 minced garlic cloves, 1 teaspoon finely chopped fresh thyme, and 2 teaspoons butter. Reduce the heat to low and simmer slowly for 10 minutes. LADLE INTO 6 SOUP BOWLS and garnish with 2 teaspoons chopped fresh mint.

lentil soup in the wintertime that I still replicate today. Another of my favorite dishes was lentils with Swiss chard. Fridays I often gave my five o'clock chocolate bar to Soeur Leila in exchange for a promise of an extra serving of lentils.

After a few months, I got used to the calm and regulated life of the convent. I enjoyed my Bible classes and often had lively arguments with my teacher, Mère de Rousiers, who was quite young and vibrant. I remember coming to the defense of Esau, who sold his birthright for a bowl of lentils. How, I argued, could he resist the pungent smell of lentils and garlic? Mère de Rousiers would laugh and say, "Colette, stop thinking with your stomach!"

It was Mère de Rousiers who often came to my defense when I was disobedient. In the convent we took baths only once a week. The bathtubs were in the basement, surrounded by curtains. The first time I bathed, I notice a large white

LENTILS WITH BEETS AND SWISS CHARD

PEEL AND DICE 3 small beets and 1 large carrot. Place in a roasting pan with 4 shallots that have been peeled and halved and drizzle with ¼ cup olive oil. Stir well. Sprinkle with salt and pepper and add 2 sprigs each fresh parsley and fresh thyme. Roast in a preheated 400-degree oven for 20 minutes.

ADD ¾ POUND French lentils and 3 cups chicken broth. Cover the pan tightly with foil and bake for 45 minutes. Remove the foil and add 1½ cups shredded Swiss chard leaves, stirring well. Bake for another 15 minutes.

STIR IN ¼ CUP OLIVE OIL, ½ teaspoon fresh lemon juice, and ¼ cup chopped parsley. Allow to cool to room temperature. This will serve 6.

sheet with a slit in it, folded carefully on the stool next to the tub. I had no idea what the sheet was for, so I simply ignored it. As I was soaking with deep pleasure in the hot water, Mère Larvulla peeked through the curtain to check on me. As soon as she saw me, she shrieked. "Mademoiselle Palacci . . . you are *never* . . . I repeat, *never* . . . to bathe in the nude! You must confess to Father Pierre." It turned out that the sheet was to be placed over the body while bathing (hence the slit for the head) to prevent a young girl from contemplating her body. I sought Mère de Rousiers' help, and she, in turn, argued for me being free of the sheet as long as I took extremely short baths. Mère Larvulla acquiesced, and from that day on, my love for Mère de Rousiers was unconditional.

I dreaded the weekends I had to go to my mother's apartment, and I was thankful that she would often call the school and tell them that my grandparents' chauffeur would pick me up instead. On her weekends, she would often send a taxi, and many a time I had to wait an hour before anyone appeared. Most of my weekends I ended up spending with my grandparents. As we lazed on the terrace, my aunts would make sly remarks to my grandmother about me being in a convent: *"Ils vont changer la petite, tu verras. Regarde-la! Elle marche déjà comme une nonne! Les gens vont parler"* ("They are going to change the girl, you'll see. Look, she already walks like a nun. People will talk"). My grandmother always defended me. "Leave the child alone! It's not her fault!" I never spoke of my life in the convent except sometimes to complain about the food. Ahmet then would prepare a care package of *sambousaks*, stuffed vine leaves, and cold sweet peppers with cheese and black olives. I would hide the package under my bed, and when the lights went out, the girls and I would jump out of bed and gather round to share these goodies.

One weekend my mother told the nuns that she had an appointment in town and sent a taxi to fetch me. When I arrived at the apartment, the maid answered the bell. I ran in looking in for my dog, Michette, and could not find her anywhere. When I asked the maid where Michette was, she answered that my mother had given my dog away, claiming that she was a nuisance. I sat in the living room waiting for my mother to come home. I don't remember what I was thinking then, but when my mother came in and found me in the dark, she asked me what was wrong. I stood up and hit her as hard as I could several times, screaming, "I hate you! I hate you! . . . You are evil! . . . You sold my dog! . . . I hate you!" My mother was taken aback by my violence and said in a small voice that was unfamiliar to me, "I am sorry . . . I just couldn't manage." But I remained unmoved. I stormed out of the room and locked myself in my bedroom. Around dinner time my mother came knocking at the door, telling me that we were going out to a nice restaurant. Would I come out? I told her to go away. As night fell, I opened the door and looked around, ready to fight again. But she had left with Hellie and Lola to go to the restaurant. I was all alone, disappointed! I went to the kitchen and made myself a sandwich, crying, "Why can't I have a mother like everyone else? I hate her!" I called my grandmother and cried on the phone. My grandmother talked to me for a long time, promising me that for the next few months I could spend all my weekends with her. I went to bed, and when my mother and Hellie came back, I refused to answer my mother's cheerful "Goodnight!" I did not speak to her for the entire weekend, even when she tried to appease me with presents. I never opened them and left them with her when I went back to school the following Monday. This silent treatment continued for weeks, but slowly, gradually, I forgot my dog.

On February 6, 1944, with my mother, Hélène, and Lola in attendance, I was baptized. Lola was my godmother—a role she took very seriously. Years later, after the war, when she lived in Belgium, she would send me cards and small presents on the anniversary of my baptism. The church that day was filled with flowers, and I felt very important. My mother explained to me that I could change my first name if I wanted to, but I was fond of the story of Sainte Colette and so decided to keep it. After the ceremony we all went out to Aboushakra, a restaurant like the one I used to go to with my grandfather, at the edge of the desert where they served grilled squab and all the things I liked to eat. This was the only time that my mother tried to please me.

Later that month I went with my mother to try on my First Communion dress. The dress was long and white with small ruffles. I also was to wear a crown of tiny flowers with a white veil. I thought I would look like a bride. My mother took me aside and told me that I shouldn't talk about any of this with my grandparents, that it would upset them. It was hard for me to understand how this event—something my mother kept telling me was the most beautiful event in the world—would hurt my grandparents. So I never said a word; I loved them too much to hurt them. Proud parents filled the church to overflowing. Mother Superior gave each new communicant a missal, and Mère de Rousiers gave me a small gold medal with the head of an angel. "I hope you will be good from now on, Colette," she said with a mischievous smile, knowing full well that I was, and always would be, in trouble with Mère Larvulla. My mother dropped from my sight for two months following the communion.

Easter vacation arrived, and my grandparents went to Alexandria. I was supposed to spend Easter vacation with my mother, but there was no word from her, so I had to remain at the convent. I was miserable. My friend Irene Tadros suggested that I come with her to Meadi, a suburb of Cairo, where her mother lived. My mother had left no instructions, and I knew that the convent would therefore not allow me to go with Irene, so we planned an escape. She would take the school bus, and I would leave the convent and take a public bus. We would meet at the railway station. I sneaked out of the building, and our plan worked. Irene's mother seemed a little puzzled that my mother had not called to announce my arrival, but she had just lost her husband, so she was happy that Irene had a friend and would be entertained.

Meadi had been developed during the war to house some of the top brass of the English army. There was a Sporting Club like the one in Cairo, and English ladies gathered at teatime in the club's garden, sipping tea. It is there that I first experienced an English high tea. We spent our days at the club's swimming pool, taking tea in the afternoon in the large garden under a white umbrella, pretending we were sophisticated ladies. We would order tea sandwiches of cucumber and tomato, hot scones with cream and strawberry jam. A few days later, my grandparents came back to Cairo. Upon learning that my mother had gone away, my grandfather sent the chauffeur to pick me up at school. I was nowhere to be found. The nuns scurried about, trying to figure out where I had gone. How could I have left the convent without anyone noticing? The police were informed, but once again, it was Mère de Rousiers who finally figured it out. She called Irene's mother and we were found. It was the only time that I heard my grandfather yell at my mother. He threatened to take me away from her if she did not take better care of me.

The convent had many holidays that we observed. One I particularly remember was the pageant of Sainte Bernadette of Lourdes. The celebration of Sainte Bernadette took place on February 15 and commemorated the poor French peasant girl who in 1848 had had eighteen visitations from the Virgin Mary in a grotto near Lourdes. At the convent, the best-behaved girl would be chosen to be Bernadette, dressed in a peasant costume to lead the procession to the grotto in the convent garden. Naturally this was a role I truly coveted. I believed that I would look perfect in a Sainte Bernadette costume, so I was confident that if I tried I could be chosen. The "competition" took place in December, when each day we behaved well we were allowed to move a little toy lamb toward the infant Jesus at the *crèche*. My lamb seemed always to be at the end of the line—I was incorrigible. Then, one night, while everyone was asleep, I crept down the staircase to the *crèche* and moved my lamb ahead of everyone else's. No one saw me; no one suspected. I repeated this every night until the day Sainte Bernadette was to be chosen, and my lamb was almost touching the baby Jesus' feet. All the girls gathered together in the large hall for the announcement. I stood there in fear, thinking I would be shamed in front of everyone. To my surprise, my name was called out as the Bernadette for that year. I was stunned and at the same time so relieved that I burst out crying. Mère de Rousiers hugged me, murmuring, "There . . . there . . . Colette! Don't cry!" For the next few weeks, I tried very hard to behave, fearing that the role of Bernadette would escape me. On the day of the procession, I was dressed in a plaid skirt with a light-sleeved blouse, a shawl around my shoulders and a scarf around my head, wooden clogs on my feet, and a basket of flowers hanging on my arm. I lead the procession and knelt in front of the grotto, look-ing—I imagined—very angelic. There is no picture of me in my costume. My mother wasn't there, and I couldn't share the event with my grandparents.

In the fall of 1947, my mother announced that we would leave Egypt for Paris. I was sad to leave, frightened of the unknown. Paris seemed so far away. I had to say goodbye to all my friends in the convent. I was hugged by Mère de Rousiers, who placed a small medal of the founding Mother in my hand. "It will protect you, Colette. Take care of yourself and don't forget us." But as much as I was sorry to leave life at the convent, which I had come to love, I was heartbroken to leave my grandparents (though I did not suspect it, I was never to see them again) and Ahmet and Aishe. During the slow boat trip to France, my mother told me that Grandmère Rose would be waiting for us in Marseilles and that for a while I should not talk about my being a Catholic or about my convent years. By then I was very religious and so once again felt confused and betrayed. But I followed my mother's lead, and while we lived with my grandmother Rose I never said a word about Catholicism.

IN 1997, I returned to Cairo with one of my own daughters—Juliette—and revisited the convent where I had spent four years of my childhood, torn between my Jewish grandparents and my Catholic mother, whose love I was so desperate for. Fifty years had gone by. The convent was no longer a boarding school but a day school. It was the last day before the summer holidays. We sat in the bright, but now shabby living room waiting for the Mother Superior. I sat as I had done years ago—stiffly on a red velvet chair that looked rather worn, under the portrait of the Sainte Mère who had founded the order a hundred years before. Little girls were running around calling to one another while their mothers tried to herd them out of the building into the waiting limousines. The nuns were no longer in formal habits but in simple day dresses and were all called Sisters. The atmosphere had lost some of its severity; everything looked casual and breezy. Suddenly the door opened, and an old nun in a navy blue dress with a white veil covering her hair came in. She

approached us and said, "I would have recognized you anywhere. You haven't changed. I am Soeur de Rousiers." We
embraced, crying like two small children. Soeur de Rousiers
was now close to eighty, but full of life. We chatted for a
while, then took a walk to the chapel. The lovely park was no
longer. The government had taken most of the land, and what
was left had been turned into a concrete playground and a
tennis court. But at the end of the yard was the grotto, still
intact with the blue statue of the Virgin Mary. I remembered
how happy and proud I had been leading that procession as
Sainte Bernadette. Suddenly I turned around to Soeur de
Rousiers and asked the question that had been on my mind
for the last fifty years. "Why was I chosen to be Sainte
Bernadette when everyone knew that I had cheated and did
not deserve it?" Soeur de Rousiers laughed and, turning to my
daughter with the same twinkle in her eyes, replied, "We all
hoped that if you were Sainte Bernadette, a miracle would
take place and you would turn into an angel!"

Today my oldest daughter Marianne has kept up some of
my Catholic practices, even though I never introduced them
into my household. She lights a candle and prays to Saint
Anthony when she wants something badly, and demonstrates
a yearning to be "good" in the Catholic tradition. And I, too,
need to reaffirm the beliefs of the little girl who was left in
the convent against her will: At Christmas we have an enormous tree surrounded by many presents. We sit around the
fireplace, sing carols, and enjoy a supper of stewed lentils,
pâté, *boudin blanc* (white pudding), a green salad, and a *bûche de
Noël* (yule-log).

CHAPTER 7

Summers

A GOLDEN SUN, DEEP BLUE WATER, LAUGHTER . . . no matter how forlorn I became during the school year, summers—from the first one I can remember—always offered a blissful hiatus from the ambiguities of belonging to everyone and to no one. My earliest memory—I must have been three—is of my French grandparents' summer house in Biarritz, a rambling villa with a large eat-in kitchen opening onto a lush herb garden. Years later when I revisited the house, I was astonished by how primitive the kitchen was.

It had a stone sink—no running hot water—and a wood-burning stove. How did Georgette, the cook and domestic *doyenne*, prepare such memorable meals there? I remember her cheeks red from the heat, and her hands smelling just like the air above the stove—of garlic, of rosemary, of ripe peaches bubbling in a tender pastry. The house was surrounded by a walled garden with espalier peach and pear trees and a grape arbor. When the bunches of grapes were ripe, my grandfather James would lift me up to snatch some. The warm grapes exploded in my mouth, and I would laugh until the front of my dress was covered with sticky juice. Grandmaman Rose would scold her husband as I scurried off to Georgette, who'd remove my dress, huffing to my grandmother, who would invariably reply: *"C'est l'été . . . laissez-la s'amuser. Je lui laverai sa robe."* ("It's summer . . . let her play. I'll wash her dress.")

Sunday lunches at Biarritz were a big affair. I would gaze with ambivalence at my aloof and stylish mother as I pressed myself up against my grandfather, who was a more obvious and reliable source of affection. Uncles, aunts, and my grandparents' friends crowded around the long table. In the morning, Georgette would have received extra help cleaning the house from the gardener and his wife. The aroma of peach or rhubarb tarts would permeate every room of the house. Hors d'oeuvre and drinks were served under an umbrella in the garden. Later, we'd feast on roast rabbit with fresh sage; tiny potatoes sautéed in duck fat; string beans or asparagus; and *pissenlit* (dandelion) salad with croutons, walnuts, and small cubes of crisp bacon. Politics dominated the discussion. I had no idea what they were talking about, although I remember hearing the word *war* repeated very often.

ROAST RABBIT WITH SAGE

RUB A 3-POUND RABBIT with salt and pepper and set it aside. Place 2 tablespoons butter, 1 tablespoon olive oil, 2 peeled garlic cloves, and 2 ounces fresh sage in a food processor and process until finely chopped. Spread this mixture all over the rabbit.

PLACE THE RABBIT in a baking pan and pour in $1/2$ cup chicken stock. Roast in a pre-heated 325-degree oven, turning often, for 1 hour, or until the rabbit is tender when pierced with a fork. Let rest for 10 minutes, then carve and serve with tiny roasted potatoes. This will serve 4.

In the afternoon the whole family would go to a pebbly beach. I preferred staying in our garden (and so avoiding my mother's scrutiny), to play with my wooden hoop or fly a small kite made by my grandfather. It didn't soar terribly high, but it had lovely drawings of cats and birds on it. In the evening my grandparents and parents would go out to dinner, and Georgette would prepare special dishes for my brother and me. I would devour the roast pullet stuffed with mushrooms, while my brother was only interested in the chocolate cake. Already he would tease me about my garlic breath . . . but I could beat him at swimming. My robust health was my best weapon against his taunting.

Before the war broke out and before my father fell ill, we joined my Egyptian grandparents and their children and grandchildren for part of the summer in Gstaad, a Swiss resort where upper-middle-class Egyptians took their families. All the children had to stay together on one floor of the hotel with their nursemaids, unpleasant for me since I was the youngest and so the natural object of the other children's jokes. I did not understand Arabic, and the older children would give me orders in Arabic that I always pretended to understand. When I then did the wrong thing, they all would laugh and expect me to cry. But I was determined not to, and within two weeks I had managed to learn enough words to more or less understand what they said. Later, when I went to live in Egypt, I learned Arabic from Aishe. One summer—I was four—my governess fell ill, so I was sent to a summer camp set on the side of a hill. I was kept busy with all the activities, and at the end of my two-week stay, we made a procession, all of us carrying lovely red paper lanterns down the

PISSENLIT [DANDELION SALAD]

WASH I POUND OF DANDELION greens or *frisée* (curly endive) and drain well. Cube 4 thick slices bacon and sauté them until well browned. Drain the bacon on paper towels and save the fat.

MIX I TABLESPOON RED WINE vinegar, $1/2$ tablespoon olive oil, and salt and pepper. Add enough of the bacon fat to make a tangy vinaigrette.

PLACE THE DANDELION GREENS in a bowl, add I cup toasted croutons, $1/2$ cup chopped walnuts, and the bacon. Toss with the vinaigrette. Serves 4 to 6.

hill and into the village. We ended up in a restaurant where we sat at long wooden tables. We were all given long-handled forks and several pieces of crispy bread to dunk in melted gruyère. I can still remember the hot, sweet, slightly nutty taste of the bubbling cheese. I would not eat fondue again until I left Cairo at the age of fifteen.

When my father was debilitated by his disease and we moved to Egypt, our summers were no longer spent in Europe. These Egyptian summers are the ones I remember most fondly; certainly they were the happiest moments of my years there. It seemed that in the summer heat, the adults were so busy trying to keep cool that they had no time to argue or to look after the younger generation. We were left to our own devices. Starting in early May, school would end at one o'clock and we would all go to the Sporting Club to swim and eat lunch. I played hide-and-seek with my young cousins among the bushes in the club's beautiful gardens while the teens took their tennis lessons.

My brother, who was two years older than me, was an awk-ward little boy, skinny, with light brown curly hair and light blue-gray eyes. He was not very handsome but was very bright. Edouard (we called him Eddy) had learned to read at four, which made my mother very proud. Eddy always had a seri-ous look on his face; my father when talking about him said, *"Il a l'air d'un vieux bonhomme"* ("He looks so grown up"). But Eddy and I did not get along. I imagine one of the reasons was that members of my family and friends would often state loudly how pretty I was but would only smile at my brother.

In July of 1939, my brother was sent back to Paris for what my mother thought was just the summer. Eddy, then ten, hated the Egyptian heat and hated even more being with my father, who was then paralyzed, and his noisy Egyptian family. We all drove through the desert to Alexandria to take my brother to the boat that would bring him to Marseilles. My French grandparents were to meet him there, and he was to return to Cairo in September. Eddy never came back. He spent the entire war in Paris, and I, who was already estranged from him emotionally, spent my youth completely separated from my only sibling.

We settled in Alexandria that summer. My grandparents had rented a large house in a new neighborhood called Smouha, not far from the racetracks since my grandfather and his sons were heavy bettors. The household included my grandparents, Tante Marie, Aishe, and me. My parents were in Upper Egypt under orders from my father's doctors. Ahmet presided over the kitchen as usual, with Abdullah helping out. We'd spend much of the day at the beach, which was defined by a half circle of elegant cabañas, each with a bar, refrigerator, table, chairs, and *chaises longues.* My grandmother and Tante Marie would settle themselves under an umbrella while Aishe and I would play in the sand. Toward noon, Ahmet and Abdullah would arrive with baskets of food. A table would be set for a glorious lunch: cold chicken with a smooth, light mayonnaise, a tomato and vegetable salad, black olives, cheeses, and a whole ice-cold sweet watermelon. After lunch both my grandparents would take a nap while I played. Ahmet and Abdullah would take the food back to the house and were given the afternoon off. Toward four o'clock, friends would join my grandparents to play cards for an hour or so while we went swimming. Some days, when it was too hot, we would return home for lunch. Later in the afternoon my grandmother and I would walk along the elegant Corniche or hire a horse-drawn carriage to take us shopping. Grandmaman loved shopping in Alexandria. She always said that going to the large department store in the Place Mohamed-Ali was like taking a trip to Paris. She'd buy French perfume, scarves, sandals, perhaps an evening dress. Summer evenings were important social events. Alexandria had elegant casinos and restaurants lining the Corniche where she and my grandfather would meet their friends for dinner and late-night gambling.

On Sundays my grandparents would rent a sailboat or a cutter, and my cousins and I would go for a long ride on the open sea. By the end of the summer I would be the color of chocolate. I never burned, which always upset my very pale cousin Renée, who'd turn into a lobster whenever she went in the sun. She had to wear a hat or stay under the umbrella with the older folks. My own mother, however, was horrified at my dark "gypsy" look. These days, I find myself admiring my eldest daughter and youngest son, who—unlike their siblings—turn brown in the summer. I also call them "gypsies" without thinking twice.

In the summer of 1942, my grandparents decided to rent a house on Ras-el-Bar, an island in the Nile Delta that is covered over by the sea during the winter months. In the summer, foundations were built and left there over the winter. In the early spring, when the sea withdrew, summer houses went up with walls made of thick straw that would let the sea breezes in. The furniture was very simple: roughly hewn wooden beds, a couple of rustic armchairs, one or two *chaises longues*. Our first summer on Ras-el-Bar, while our house was being built, we stayed at the Grand Hotel Aslan. Despite its pretentious name, it was built of the same materials as the private houses and was just as primitive. I was in my own private heaven. I could run around barefoot all day, dressed either in my bathing suit or in a light summer dress. When the Nile flooded—which was at the end of the summer—crabs could be caught simply by scooping them out of the shallow water along the shore. Every Saturday night, an enormous trestle table was set on the beach in front of the verandah and cov-

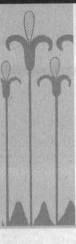

BOILED BLUE CRABS WITH GINGER SCALLION SAUCE

BRING 2 QUARTS OF WATER to a boil in a very large saucepan or pot. Add 12 peppercorns, 1 tablespoon coarse salt, and 2 bay leaves. Boil for 2 minutes, then add 12 live blue crabs and cook for 8 minutes. Drain and cool.

PEEL A 4-INCH PIECE of fresh ginger and cut it into small pieces. Place it in a food processor with 4 chopped scallions, 1 cup vegetable oil, and salt and pepper. Process until well puréed, place in a bowl to serve as a dipping sauce for the crabs. Twelve crabs will serve 4.

ered with mounds of steamed crabs and bowls of different sauces to dip the crab meat in; bright red tomato salads with lots of garlic; chickpea salad with red onions and thin slices of broiled eggplant soaking in pungent olive oil; crisp French bread; ice-cold beer; and lemonade for the children. Most of the time, people stood around the table eating and chatting. The older people sat on chairs with their plates on their knees. Children would run around, picking up a crab leg here and there. I took my crustacean eating seriously and did no running around but rather sat solemnly over my pile of crabs, cracking the shells with my teeth. I can still hear my grandmother's voice intoning, over and over, "Careful, Colette, you are going to break a tooth!" I never did. I still crack crab shells with my teeth, but when I see my children and grandchildren following suit, I admonish them just as my grandmother did.

That summer I made a friend named Nadine. We were inseparable. Nadine had an older brother, Jacques, who was about fourteen years old and was only interested in girls slightly older than he. Often Nadine and I would follow him around, making jokes about the girls he wanted to impress. He spent most of his time trying to chase us away. I think I had a crush on him, but he ignored me completely. However, one late August morning, Nadine came running to me telling me to join her and her brother to see the flooding of the Nile. One side of the island of Ras-el-Bar faces the open sea, while the other side faces the Nile Delta. We stood on the edge of the water, looking at the delta. I saw nothing out of the ordinary. The water was blue and calm, as usual, and I was about to leave when suddenly I saw the massive river literally cut through the sea. A narrow body of brown water was slowly advancing through the greenish blue of the ocean water like a giant liquid eel until the two waters began to mingle. As the Nile advanced, schools of fish churned the water in a frenzy to swim toward the open sea. Jacques told us to get into the water and showed us how to catch fish with our bare hands. He had brought a basket, and within ten minutes it was full of quivering fish, which we brought to Nadine's house. Her mother invited me to stay for a dinner of mounds of fried fish and a big green salad. The next day I was told two disappointing things—that we could no longer go into the sea

FRIED FISH WITH GROUND
ALMOND-ANCHOVY SAUCE

MARINATE 12 SMALL PORGIES, butterfish, or other small seafish in a mixture of ¹/₂ cup olive oil, 2 chopped onions, the juice of 1 lemon, 2 tablespoons chopped fresh thyme, 1 tablespoon chopped fresh marjoram, and salt and pepper for 1 hour.

MEANWHILE, TURN 1 SMALL CAN of anchovies with their oil into a mortar and pound with the pestle until smooth. Heat 2 tablespoons vegetable oil in a skillet and add 3 crushed garlic cloves; sauté for 2 minutes. Add the anchovy paste and 1 tablespoon flour. Stir well, then add ¹/₂ cup white wine vinegar and ³/₄ cup water, stirring all the while. Add ¹/₂ cup ground almonds and 2 tablespoons tomato paste diluted in ¹/₂ cup water. Bring to a boil, lower the heat, and simmer for 20 minutes, stirring from time to time. Place in a bowl and garnish with 2 tablespoons chopped fresh parsley.

SEASON 1 CUP of flour with salt and pepper. Heat 2¹/₂ cups olive oil in a large skillet. Coat a few fish with the flour and fry in very hot oil until golden on each side. Drain on paper towels, then transfer to the oven to keep warm. Serve the sauce with the fish. This will serve 4.

as it was contaminated with dead fish, and besides it was time to return to Cairo. The straw walls of the summer houses would be rolled up and sent to the mainland for storage. By the time the boat came to pick us up, Ras-el-Bar would look like a ghost town, and soon the foundations of the houses would be covered by floodwaters.

I was twelve and a half in the summer of 1944, and my mother announced to my grandparents that I was to attend camp rather than go to the island. She thought that I spent too much time in the company of adults and that I should spend the summer with children my own age. I was devastated by the prospect of missing another carefree summer by the delta and begged my grandfather to say no. Although he agreed with my mother, he compromised and insisted that I spend the month of August back with the family. And so in June, after the closing of the school, Aishe embroidered my name on everything she thought I would take with me: handkerchiefs that I never used, socks that I never wore, even ribbons that I had no need for since I kept my hair tightly braided.

On July 1, a bus crammed with children ranging in age from ten to fifteen years old came to the front door to pick me up for camp. There was only one seat left for me, near a boy with black unruly hair falling over his eyes. The first hour, no one talked despite the counselor's efforts to get us to sing and tell stories. An hour later, lunchboxes were handed out containing uninspired cheese sandwiches and a piece of fruit. As usual, Ahmet had prepared for me a care package with tomato, feta, and black olive sandwiches; homemade potato chips; slices of mango; and his famous walnut cookies. I was embarrassed and did not know if I should open the box on my lap. Suddenly the black-haired boy asked, "So what's in that box?"

I smiled. "Would you like to share it? Our cook prepared it. He's always afraid I'll starve because I usually don't like food that he doesn't prepare."

"What's your name?" I asked.

"Henri Dufour. I'm fourteen. I have three other brothers. In front is Carl, the blond one. He's twelve. Then there's André; he's eleven. He's sitting in the back. André likes girls. The youngest one is Philippe; he's nine. What's your name? Can I have that sandwich?"

I was dumbfounded, speechless, as I handed him my sandwich. His eyes were deep, dark blue and he had a dimple on one side of his cheek when he smiled. "What's your name?" he asked gruffly. "Don't you have a tongue?" I finally caught my breath. "Colette," I answered. I was in love and knew that I wanted to spend the whole summer with him.

During the long ride to Alexandria, Henri talked about his father, who was with de Gaulle in London. "He's fighting the Nazis. He's going to liberate France," he proclaimed proudly. His mother stayed in Cairo and worked for the French radio, trying every day to get in touch with his father. This was his first time at summer camp. He only went to help look after his younger brothers. "I'm too old to be in a children's camp," he said disdainfully. He talked the entire trip. I only nodded, agreeing to whatever he said. I dreaded our arrival, believing that our budding friendship would dissolve as soon as the bus reached camp.

The camp was set on an arid spit of land outside of Alexandria near the sea. There were separate bungalows for girls and boys with a large swimming pool in between, tennis courts, and sailboats. I shared a bungalow with four other girls about my age. That first night I could not sleep, worrying if I would be with Henri again. The next morning in the mess hall where breakfast was served, Henri spied me and motioned to come and sit next to him and his brothers. I was introduced to his brothers as his friend Colette. "She comes with us," he told them with the authority only an older brother can command. Carl, who seemed about to object to the presence of a girl in their very masculine midst, met with Henri's sharp glance and nodded his head vigorously in agreement. I learned very quickly that whenever Henri spoke, the boys—and soon I—obeyed. When he decided that we should volunteer for the sailing class, we all did, although I hated sailing because I was often seasick. I had to go on long hikes, although I did not like walking in the heat. One morning Henri decided that all five of us would enter the swimming competition. I was a good swimmer but had my doubts about competing among older campers. Henri looked at me and simply said, in his gruff voice, "We'll practice." We—or rather, I—practiced for a couple of hours a day until I could even beat Carl, who was a very fast swimmer. At night I would lay awake imagining Henri saying something nice to me like in the novels I had started to read. What would it be like to be kissed by him? Did he love me as I loved him?

The day of the competition arrived, and I knew that I had to win if I wanted Henri to love me and be proud of me. The first two races were easy and I won. The last one was more difficult. I was competing with girls taller and stronger than I. I don't remember how I won, but I did, and as I lifted myself out of the water, Henri hugged me hard without saying a word. I was pleased but had hoped for a kiss.

Once more, food played a crucial role in my relationships. I hated the food in the camp and always waited impatiently for Ahmet's care package, which arrived every week full of treats: Italian salami, cheeses, cookies, dates. I naturally shared them with all four brothers, which helped me get on better with Carl, who did not approve of my being part of their group. I also soon discovered that Henri and his brothers ate whatever was put in front of them but that they were always hungry for more. And so I became the provider. I would pile my plate with mashed potatoes, meat or fish, and several pieces of bread. I would take only a couple of bites from my overflowing plate and then share the rest with the boys. This happened regularly, except on the days we went shrimp fishing. I loved the tiny shrimp. All the children waded in the water with a small bucket next to them. The sea was full of shrimp and scooping them up into our nets was very easy. We would all bring our catch to the kitchen, and that night they would be served for dinner—just boiled, with olive oil as a dip. It was the only time that Carl would reciprocate and give me his share—not out of kindness but because he loathed shrimp.

A few days before the end of camp, there was to be a dance. Henri immediately announced that he hated dancing. "It's for sissies," he barked. I was stricken with disappointment. Still, I put on the white linen dress that Grandmaman had made me. I thought I looked lovely. Henri, of course, was nowhere to be seen. Carl was in a corner sulking, and André was dancing with a bevy of girls. A few boys asked me to dance, and I had started to enjoy myself when Henri appeared at the door. When the music stopped, I went nonchalantly up to him, trying to look bored by the whole event. Henri whispered, "Would you like to go for a walk with me?" I followed him without speaking, and we found ourselves on the beach. Suddenly Henri took my hand and held it tightly. I was afraid to move or say anything. We stood for what seemed to me an eternity, but which was probably just a few minutes. Then Henri bent down and kissed me, a quick peck on the lips. I blurted out, "I love you," and to my amazement, he answered, "Me too." We slowly walked back in silence, holding hands.

The next few days were bliss. Henri never left my side. I was now his "girlfriend." He asked me to go on walks with him, and we would stroll hand in hand on the beach. Once he picked up a lovely pink shell and gave it to me. I have it still. When we went sailing, he made sure I sat near him. His brothers were astonished to see the change. Once Carl made a joke about me and Henri got very angry with him. For a day Carl sat all by himself, ignored by his brothers, but I made sure that we made peace, as I missed being one of the boys. At the end of the month, most of the campers, including the Dufour brothers, took the bus back to Cairo. I was going to join my grandparents in Alexandria. Henri promised to write. He lived in Meadi, and it was too far for him to come and see me during the school year, so he promised he would see me the following summer. I did not see him or hear from him for the whole year, and I was too shy to write. But when the summer vacation discussion came up, I insisted, to everyone's astonishment, that I be sent again to summer camp.

As I saw the bus approaching to pick me up, I got panicky and was sorry that I had insisted on going to camp and not with my grandparents and cousins to Marsa Matruk, the new resort about an hour from Alexandria where they had built a house. What if Henri were not there? Or if another girl sat next to him? As I climbed on the bus, I saw with despair that the Dufour boys were not in it. I rode in silence all the way to Alexandria. Once settled in my bungalow, I tried to find out why the Dufour brothers were not attending. I was told that their mother had gone to Port Said, taking her children with her. I was crestfallen. I had dreamed all winter long about our being together in camp. Everywhere I went, there was a reminder of how happy I had been the summer before. I replayed in my mind his last words and his promise to be with me the following summer. After a few days in camp, I was determined not to stay. I called my grandparents and told them how miserable I was. "You have to stay," my grandfather said in a stern voice. I asked to speak with my grandmother and whispered, "The food is horrible. I can't eat anything." As I had lost a lot of weight the previous summer, my grand-mother took my side, and within forty-eight hours my grand-parents' chauffeur picked me up and drove me to Marsa Matruk. A few years later, when I returned to Paris to live, I searched for Henri's number in the telephone book and found that the name Dufour was as common in France as Smith is in America. I tried a few Dufours, but none had been in Cairo during the war.

Marsa Matruk was a long and wide stretch of beach that had been purchased by my grandfather and a small group of other businessmen. Our bungalow, built right on the beach, was unusually simple. The water in the kitchen and bathroom smelled strongly of sulfur, and drinking water came in large green bottles from the city. Behind the house was a field of fig trees. In the morning, a young Arab boy would walk among the houses shouting, *"Teen! Teen!"* (Arabic for figs). Ahmet served the green figs neatly peeled with slices of feta or *eishta*, rich Turkish coffee, and very thin, toasted Arab bread. For lunch, we had grilled chicken marinated in lime and served with roasted bananas, ice-cold watermelon, and more figs. We spent the day in and out of the water, playing volleyball, running on the beach, or taking long, lazy walks. At the end of the day, my skin would be coated with a fine layer of powdery sand

GRILLED CHICKEN WITH ROASTED BANANAS

To make this dish you really need very small chickens, no more than 2½ pounds each. Small bananas, about 4 inches long and 1½ inches in diameter, are best. They are available in many specialty grocers. Sumac is available in Indian stores.

CHOP 1 LARGE ONION and squeeze the pieces through a garlic press into a large bowl. Mix with the juice of 3 limes, 3 tablespoons olive oil, 1 tablespoon sumac, 3 finely chopped garlic cloves, and salt and pepper. Halve 2 small chickens; turn the chicken several times in the marinade to coat; cover and refrigerate overnight.

PREPARE A CHARCOAL GRILL. Grill the chicken halves, turning frequently and brushing with the marinade, until done. Remove to a platter. Peel 4 small bananas and dip them in the marinade. Grill the bananas 3 minutes per side, and serve with the chicken.

THE BEST ACCOMPANIMENT is a salad of cucumbers and yogurt. Serves 4.

that hid my deep tan, and I reveled in my hair, which was bleached blond in the sun.

It is in Marsa Matuck that I enjoyed my first glass of wine. We were sitting on the terrace of the house, our faces glowing in the candlelight. One of my cousins brought out a bottle of red wine. I was twelve and a half and thought of myself as a grownup. When wine was poured all around, I picked up a glass, said, *"À votre santé,"* in a joyful voice with a hint of defi-

ance, and drank the entire contents. I coughed violently, choking on the dry wine, and everyone laughed. My grandfather
clucked disapprovingly, but from that night on, I was granted
a glass of wine every night.

When my mother announced in 1947 that we would go
back to Paris, everyone around me said how lucky I was to
leave Egypt for France. So I was only slightly disappointed not
to go once again to the beach house. As it happened, leaving
Cairo would transform my life forever.

Paris was a city recovering from four years of Nazi occupation. We stayed in my grandmother's apartment. My grandfather had died of pneumonia in 1945, just as the war ended.
He might have lived if medicine could have been found, but
in those last few weeks one could not find any medicine, not
even in the black market. I spent that summer studying so I
could enter a French *lycée* in the fall. My grandmother Rose
found me too wild and unruly for her taste. My brother,
whom I had not seen for eight years, treated me like an
intruder. He was angry because I had had a joyful time in
Cairo while he lived under the German occupation. He had
been afraid of being caught by the Nazis and sent to a camp.
Since he had an Egyptian passport and Egypt was secretly an
ally of the Germans, he had not worn the yellow star that all
Jews wore at that time. My grandparents were never bothered
by the Germans because my grandfather, I learned later, had
at the age of eighteen changed his name to Bémant and never
told anyone he was a Jew. In the apartment house where they
lived, everyone, including the concierge, thought they were
Catholics. This was fortunate for concierges were, during the
occupation, more often than not, the ones who would
denounce tenants to the Germans.

I missed Ahmet and Aishe, the food, the sunshine, and above all my Egyptian grandparents and the large house. That winter, my mother left me in Paris and returned to Cairo, promising that the following summer I would be back on the beach of Marsa Matruck. I tried that winter to become what my grandmother Rose called *"une jeune fille de bonne famille."* My Egyptian accent disappeared. I learned to tame my curly hair, to wear heels, to dress well. I also learned about French cuisine, and how to eat an artichoke daintily. I discovered *gigot d'agneau, haricots verts,* and *morelles.* Still, when I ate a ballottine of duck, the dish would bring back memories of Ahmet's kitchen and I would feel totally forlorn. In Egypt, even if I was often lonely, there was noise, family laughter, and a loving grandmother. Our house in Paris was dark and silent, my grandmother Rose did not encourage me to bring friends home, and for the first two years I was not allowed to go out on my own.

That first summer after my return to Paris, I was told I would accompany my mother's family to the south of France, not go back to Alexandria as I had been promised. My French grandmother, my mother (who had returned from Cairo for a short period), my brother, and I settled down in Cannes in a hotel far from the beach. There was no more running around barefoot, eating when and what we wanted. I hated that summer of 1948. I missed the laughter and wonderful spirit of my Egyptian family. I would never see my Egyptian grandparents again. My grandfather Vita died in 1955, and my grandmother Marguerite soon after. I did not know then that it would be another twenty-five years before I would return to my beloved Cairo.

CHAPTER 8

The Return

I SPENT THE NEXT SIX YEARS, UNTIL 1955 WHEN I
left to get married at age twenty-three, with
my maternal grandmother in her apartment
on the avenue de la Grande Armée in Paris,
the same one I had left when I was five. My
grandfather James had died in 1945, the year
the war was over, and after a few months in
Paris my mother decided to go back to Egypt.
She did not get along with her mother, and
the difficulties of everyday life were such a
strain for her. This was another in her long
line of periodic abandonments of me. I

shared the large dwelling with my grandmother Rose and my brother. His bedroom—called the bachelor's room because it had its own entrance—allowed discreet visits and exits. In great contrast to my airy, simply furnished Cairo bedroom, my Paris bedroom was ornate, with a heavy four-poster bed, silk draperies, a *chaise longue*, and narrow windows from which I could see the Arc de Triomphe. To get away from my rather strict grandmother, I could usually be found in my grandfather's study, curled up in a deep leather armchair with a book, or doing my homework at his carved mahogany desk, which stood solidly in the corner.

That fall, I was fifteen and was registered at the Lycée la Fontaine, a new, modern high school built near to the Bois de Boulogne. The *lycée* was also near an Olympic-sized open-air swimming pool. On days when I felt depressed, I would cut school and go swimming. From the first day I attended school I was nicknamed *l'Egyptienne* (the Egyptian girl), an epithet that stung me deeply, for I desperately wanted to fit in. Although I missed my Egyptian grandparents and our way of life in Cairo, I made a point to become as French as quickly as I could. Not half French, half Egyptian. I needed to be whole. So I shed my accent, as well as excess pounds, and wore a navy blue dress with a white collar like all the other girls in my class. I rode a bicycle, ate a *sandwich au jambon* for lunch, and spent hours with my new friends discussing Sartre and Simone de Beauvoir. I never spoke about food—my passion—nor about my years in Egypt, especially if my brother was around. He resented the "privileged" childhood I had had while he was living through the German occupation, with its food shortages and the fear of being caught by the Nazis. Both he and my grandmother would stare at me coldly and say, "You don't understand anything. You weren't here." I felt guilty for having been away, ashamed of being Catholic; in their eyes, that was the ultimate betrayal on my part. But how could I erase four years of my life and pretend they never happened? I tried. I hid my missal, never went to church, and desperately feigned interest in Jewish history. Most of the time, though, I was miserable. Today, I still don't know what I am. I feel ambivalence toward both religions. I haven't been to church in years. I don't feel Jewish but feel very protective of anything Jewish. I sometimes think I have failed my children because I have given them the same ambivalence toward being Jewish as I have.

My only pleasure during the first two years back in Paris was being with Georgette in the kitchen. Though much had changed, Georgette was still queen of the kitchen, and the smells of her cooking enchanted and fascinated me. They were so different from Ahmet's: instead of cumin and cardamom lingering in the air, there was garlic and parsley, fresh basil and wine. Now that Georgette was maid and chauffeur as well as cook, my grandmother allowed me—even encouraged me—to help Georgette in the kitchen after school. (Was I no longer *une jeune fille de bonne famille?*) The bounty of the morning's market was placed on an enamel-top table, which was often covered with a checkered oilcloth. While I trimmed string beans or peeled potatoes, Georgette talked to me about the war years, when she would cycle several kilometers outside Paris to her brother's house to get some food for our family. She told me she stayed with my grandparents because she loved my grandfather so much. He was, she said, a very kind man who had hired her at the age of sixteen and would not allow my grandmother to boss her around. "Did I tell you that he wanted me to go back to school? I said no because I was afraid. Now I regret it! He was always giving me things to read." She would have liked to have married, but she felt she could not leave my grandparents alone during the war, and now she was too old. In turn, I told her about Aishe and Ahmet, about the mango tree outside my window, and about my stay in the convent. As we chatted, I was learning how to make a perfect vinaigrette, mayonnaise from scratch, roux

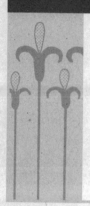

TOMATO SALAD

PEEL AND SLICE 4 ripe tomatoes. Place in a salad bowl.

MIX TOGETHER 1 MINCED SHALLOT, 1 tablespoon chopped fresh tarragon, 1 tablespoon chopped chives, 1 tablespoon fresh lemon juice, 2½ tablespoons olive oil, and salt and pepper. Beat with a whisk until emulsified and pour over the tomatoes. Toss and serve. This is enough for 4.

without a single lump, paper-thin crêpes—in short, all the basics of French cuisine—without even realizing it. It never occurred to me until the day my grandmother, who never paid me any compliments, grudgingly acknowledged that my tomato salad was the best she had ever tasted.

My father, just before he died, had named trustees to take care of my brother and me. He also appointed his younger brother, Clement, as my guardian. During the war, my Egyptian grandparents were responsible for me, but once I arrived in Paris, my uncle took over. He was a charming bachelor without any idea of how to care for a teenage girl. Each time I expressed my unhappiness with my life at my grandmother's house, and my intense desire to return to Egypt, he'd shove a wad of French *franc* notes into my hand and say, "*Tiens, va t'amuser. Achete-toi une jolie robe*" ("Here, go have fun. Buy yourself a pretty dress"). I would take the money and hide it in the back flap of my diary, with the intention of saving enough money to run away to Egypt when I was eighteen. Unfortunately, sooner or later I would end up shopping; in the end I saved very little.

Everything changed in 1948, the year of my sixteenth birthday. That June, Georgette got the flu; this turned into pneumonia, and she died in three weeks. I thought then that I would not survive. Only Georgette had showed me any love. I was convinced that no one else would listen to my stories or console me when I felt blue. I was silent for days; even weeks later I remained withdrawn with my morbid thoughts. Then in early July, the youngest son of an American friend of my grandparents came to stay with us for a few days, and my grandmother gave me the task of showing him Paris. James was tall, handsome, and much older than I was (twenty-one seemed rather ancient to me), with an irresistible lock of dark brown hair cascading over his forehead and his left eye. He was enchanted with Paris, more so than any visitor I had ever met. He walked the streets all day long, a sketchbook under one arm, seemingly oblivious of me, his tour guide who trailed behind him (his legs were twice as long as mine). He would stop in front of a church or a small square and start to draw. We talked very little; I was shy about speaking English, and he knew no French. After one week I was madly in love. He said years later that he fell in love with me on the first evening we met, because I served him the best tomato salad he had ever eaten.

I was devastated when he left to continue his tour of France, Sweden, and Italy. I thought I would never see him again. My grandmother, who was truly touched by my sorrow, took me to Hendaye, a little town on the Atlantic coast, where the beach reminded me of Alexandria. I was fond of the small *auberge* that overlooked the sea and the excellent Basque food served there: skate sautéed with tomatoes and hot peppers, squid cooked in its own ink, hearty bean soup, a fricassée of fennel. Not even my enjoyment of good food could assuage

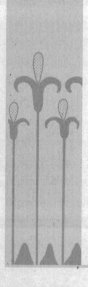

SKATE WITH PEPPERS

Skate should be filleted and skinned by the fishmonger, who should also be able to sell you fish stock for this dish.

CUT 2 RED BELL PEPPERS and 2 green bell peppers into 1-inch strips. Heat 1 tablespoon olive oil in a large skillet and sauté 1 minced garlic clove for a minute. Add the peppers and sauté for 4 minutes, stirring with a wooden spoon. Season with salt and pepper and 2 tablespoons chopped fresh oregano. Set aside in the skillet.

PLACE 3 POUNDS OF SKATE fillets in a large skillet. Cover with boiling fish stock. Bring to a boil, then lower the heat and simmer for 8 minutes. Remove the fish with slotted spoons and place on top of the peppers. Heat through.

TRANSFER THE FISH and peppers to a platter. Garnish with 2 tablespoons capers and 1 can rolled anchovies, sprinkle with 2 tablespoons chopped fresh parsley, and serve. This will serve 4 to 6.

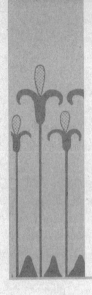

BEAN SOUP

COVER I CUP DRIED NAVY BEANS with water and soak overnight.

DRAIN THE BEANS and place in a large saucepan with I onion stuck with 2 cloves, 6 crushed garlic cloves, and 8 cups chicken stock. Bring to a boil, lower the heat, and simmer for 2 hours or until tender.

ADD ½ CUP OF PEELED, seeded, and diced tomatoes, ½ cup chopped fresh parsley, ½ cup of mixed chopped fresh sage and thyme, ¼ cup olive oil, ½ pound cubed Spanish sausage (*chorizo*), and salt and pepper. Cook for 8 minutes.

LADLE INTO 6 SOUP BOWLS and garnish with toasted croutons.

my pain, however, and I pined openly for the young American, much to my stern grandmother's consternation and annoyance. At the end of our first week, just as my mouth was beginning to take on a permanent pinch, I received a telegram. James had decided to abandon his travels to join us in Hendaye. The next three weeks were out of a Victorian novel. We were inseparable and became adept at escaping my grandmother's disapproving—and almost all-seeing—eye. James proposed to me and I accepted, and being the naive sixteen-year-old that I was, I blurted this out to the person who had the least trust in my maturity—my grandmother. She immediately asked him to leave, and none of my ranting could change her opinion—shared by my guardian uncle—of this *scandale.* James promised me passionately that he would come

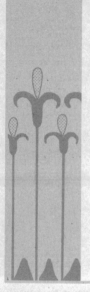

FRICASSEE OF FENNEL

WASH, TRIM, AND QUARTER 4 fennel bulbs.
HEAT 4 TABLESPOONS BUTTER in a saucepan.
Add ¼ pound peeled pearl onions and ¼ pound
diced bacon. Cook over medium heat until the
bacon is nearly crisp. Remove with a slotted
spoon and reserve. Add the fennel to the
saucepan and sauté for 5 minutes. Return the
bacon and onions to the pan, lower the heat, and
simmer for 10 minutes.

HEAT ¼ CUP OLIVE OIL in a large skillet. Add
6 small potatoes that have been peeled and quartered, and sauté for 10 minutes. Add the fennel
mixture and season with salt and pepper. Pour in
½ cup chicken stock and simmer for 20 minutes,
or until the potatoes are tender. Sprinkle with
1½ tablespoons chopped fresh rosemary. This
will serve 6.

back for me after he had finished college and his architectural
studies, a vow that sustained me for the next six years. We
were married in 1955, and I left France for good.

Being French, however, was a distinct advantage in New
York City. My Egyptian "half" made me seem even more
exotic to Americans just beginning to be interested in things
foreign. For the first time in five years, I could speak openly
about Cairo. James and I settled in an old town house. Its narrow, galley-style kitchen became my domain; no longer would
I be a visitor hanging around the fringes of the kitchen. At
first, I found shopping a baffling and stressful experience. I
didn't recognize any of the cuts of meat sold at the supermar-

ket, everything was wrapped in plastic, and the only salad I could find was iceberg lettuce. I was equally dismayed at the food I was served at other people's houses: shredded carrots entombed in trembling green Jell-O, ham covered with brown sugar and canned pineapple, overgrown and overcooked vegetables, noodles mixed with canned tuna fish and globs of mayonnaise out of jars. Rather than the full midday meal I was used to, I had to content myself with soggy, gummy cream cheese and chive sandwiches, which I despised—and still do. I lost weight immediately until I discovered hamburgers, which I thought were quite delicious. What distressed me most was the white, soft, utterly tasteless packaged bread sold in my neighborhood. All this changed when I discovered the immigrant neighborhoods of the Lower East Side, Little Italy, and Bleeker Street in Greenwich Village, each a distinct cultural gem in a city I was slowly falling in love with.

Once I found out that New York had butcher shops, I began to try to reproduce some of the dishes I had seen Georgette make in Paris. On Sundays I served a roast leg of lamb, medium rare, studded with slivers of garlic and covered with fresh herbs. I made quiche, cheese soufflé, lamb stew, and steak with *pommes frites* (French fries) the French way, cherry fondant. I bought hand-churned butter and fresh farmer's cheese from a Jewish dairy, and I served rich chocolate mousse and open fruit tartes to my guests. I even called Paris to find out how to make crème fraîche. American eating habits continued to shock me, but I learned to love baked potatoes, steamed lobster, clam chowder, barbecued spareribs, and Good Humor ice cream bars.

When I began to shop along Atlantic Avenue in Brooklyn, a wide street lined with Syrian and Lebanese food shops and restaurants, I finally felt that New York was my home. The first time I entered one of these shops, I was transported back to Cairo and shopping with Ahmet for that night's dinner. Here were barrels of dried beans, small green lentils, split peas, *ful medames,* all manner of olives, preserved lemons, pickled onions, and *torchi* (turnips pickled in brine and beet juice). I stared at the piles of pita bread, chunks of Kashkaval cheese, and sheets of dried apricot paste that in Cairo my schoolmates and I used to wrap around a piece of ice and suck on when the weather was very hot. The owner greeted me in Arabic, and to my amazement, I responded; I had not spoken Arabic in years. On that day, I bought a little of everything, but when I returned to my kitchen, I realized that I had almost no idea of how to prepare the dishes of my childhood. I tried to *be* Ahmet, but the *ful* was mushy, the *mulukhiyya* soup watery

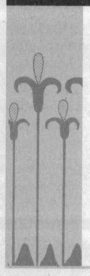

ROAST LEG OF LAMB

TRIM A 5½-POUND LEG OF LAMB of excess fat. Cut 4 garlic cloves into slivers, use the point of a knife to make deep holes in the lamb, and insert the garlic slivers. Season well with salt and pepper and place in a baking pan. Sprinkle with 2 tablespoons chopped fresh tarragon and dot with 4 tablespoons butter. Pour ½ cup water into the bottom of the pan and place in a preheated 350-degree oven. For medium rare, bake 15 minutes per pound; for medium, 20 minutes per pound. Allow the meat to rest 20 minutes before carving. Serve with your favorite potatoes (I would serve *pommes Anna*) and a salad. This will serve 6 to 8.

CHERRY FONDANT

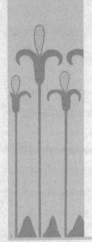

SEPARATE 4 LARGE EGGS and pit 1 pound Bing cherries.

PLACE THE YOLKS in a food processor with 1 cup sugar and ½ teaspoon cinnamon and process for 1 minute.

CUT 1 POUND BUTTER into pieces. Reserve 1 tablespoon for the mold and melt the rest. With the processor running, pour the melted butter into the egg yolk mixture. Add 1¾ cups all-purpose flour and process for 30 seconds. Turn the dough out into a bowl.

WHIP THE EGG WHITES with a pinch of salt until stiff. Gently fold the whites into the dough. Butter a one-quart mold and spoon in the dough. Top with the cherries (some will sink) and bake in a preheated 375-degree oven until a knife inserted in the middle comes out clean, about 40 minutes.

COOL ON A RACK, unmold, and serve at room temperature. This is enough for 6.

and bland, and the *tehina* cementlike in consistency and taste. So I went back to Atlantic Avenue and spoke to store owners and restaurant cooks. I took down recipes, experimented, and within a few weeks I served my first real Egyptian dinner: smooth *tehina* with toasted pita; vine leaves stuffed with chopped lamb and rice, served with yogurt; *mulukhiyya* with rice; grilled squab with okra and tomatoes; and baklava. To my great relief, my children relished the food, and from then on, once a month I would prepare an Egyptian meal. I told them bedtime stories about my youthful adventures in Cairo. The one they liked the best was my story of being the great-great-great-granddaughter of a princess. I thought a small white lie would not hurt.

My daughter Marianne thought she looked like my Egyptian grandmother (she does), and took as her own all of Grandmaman's superstitions; my son, Thomas, accepted his very curly hair, calling it his "Arab inheritance." Juliette loved the food and became seriously interested in the Middle East, and Cecile decided to dress up as an Egyptian princess at the school's Halloween party. Egypt was once again part of my life.

As the years went by, my desire to go back to Egypt grew stronger. I also started to question my memories. Was the house as large as I imagined? Did the mango tree really exist? Were the exciting tensions of cultural differences apparent in the streets of Cairo? In its cuisine? In its people? My Egyptian relatives had long ago moved back to Paris; they skirted my questions; their answers were vague. After all, they had lost their fortunes during the revolution of 1952, in which the king was ousted and Egypt declared a republic, and they no longer thought of Egypt as a home or a haven. Their children and grandchildren were French, they insisted; I should forget the past. *"Laisse tomber!"* ("Drop it!"), they told me repeatedly. My mother, who had followed us to New York in 1965 was no help, tending to dwell on her very early years as a Parisian *ingénue.* The more they denied the stories of my past, the more I wanted to return. In 1979, my husband was hired by the United Nations to help design the new capital of Tanzania in East Africa. He was told that he had to spend several months there and that he could take his family along. Since Cairo was a stop on the way, my husband offered me a trip there. I decided that my son Thomas, about eleven at the time, would accompany us, since his sisters were at college.

We arrived at the bustling, dusty Cairo airport and chose a taxi. Our first stop, I insisted, would not be our hotel, but my childhood home. I gave the driver the address on Ismail Pacha Street, and as he slowed down in front of a house and pointed, I burst into tears. "No, no . . . that's not it! It's a big house with a mango tree in the garden. Where's the gate with the huge brass *P*'s?" My husband interrupted me and said that I could be mistaken, that my memories could be wrong. Perhaps I might only have remembered my house as large. I would not listen, and told the driver that this was not my street nor was it my house, and to drive us back to the hotel. I was inconsolable and could not sleep. Were my memories so wrong? Did I invent those images that haunted me and made my heart burn with nostalgia?

About seven o'clock the next morning a telephone call woke us up. It was the taxi driver from the night before. He was bursting with excitement; he had found the house! We dressed quickly and drove with him. There was the house, with its gate, the mango tree, and the large terrace. As we rang the bell, a tall man in a *galabeyya* and turban answered. This was Ahmet's son, who was living there as caretaker for the bank that now owned it. While I was able to reminisce with him about Ahmet, I was unable to walk through my old house. The bank denied me permission. I was disappointed, but at least now Thomas and my husband would bear the good news to my other children that their mother's stories had not been invented!

We spent only three days in Cairo. We had ice cream at Groppi's, which was not as elegant as I remembered; we went to the City of the Dead to see the tombs; we ate *ful* and *lokoumadis* in the street and had grilled pigeon and stuffed grape leaves for dinner. We drank mango and sweet lemon juice and munched on sugarcane. On the second night we drove to the Pyramids and went looking for the village where my grandfather used to rent camels. With sheer luck, we found it, and the same family was still there renting camels. We went galloping into the desert to the Sphinx under a sky filled with stars that inspired Thomas with the same awe I had felt when I had gone galloping in the desert as a ten-year-old. We were tiny humans lost under an immense black sky filled with mystery.

Now, when I think of those lost days in Egypt, I am happy and secure in my memories. Now, when I watch my daughter Juliette sitting in the kitchen rolling grape leaves, I recall myself fondly: the small girl with curly hair sitting on a stool looking at Ahmet doing the same thing. And the ties are not severed: My son Thomas shops on Atlantic Avenue. My daughter Cecile, who is living in Berlin, calls me in New York for Egyptian recipes. Today, my grandson Matthew loves *ful* as much as I do, and he thinks that *mulukhiyya* is "cool."

In 1997, my daughter Juliette, a reporter, had to interview a famous billionaire in Cairo and asked me if I'd like to accompany her. I jumped at the idea. We put up at the Nile Hilton, a new hotel overlooking the Nile. As I stood at my window, I felt a pang of sadness. What I was looking at were modern twenty-story buildings, elevated roadways, and, in the distance, speedboats crossing the Nile. I thought then that I had made a mistake. The Cairo I knew was gone. Cairo was a modern city with all the problems of a Third World capital that had grown too fast. More women covered their heads with scarfs, but on the other hand, as I sat in the hotel restaurant near the pool, I saw women smoking the *chichah* (water pipe) in public, which was unthinkable when I was young.

The next day, I took a taxi with Juliette and asked the driver to take us to Ismail Pasha Street in Garden City. We roamed for twenty minutes through the neighborhood, which I no longer recognized. We asked doormen, police, passersby, but no one seemed to know where the street was. I felt discouraged and angry with myself for having come to Cairo. Later that afternoon, we visited the Khan-al-Khalili market. And at least there I could walk through the streets and find a taste of my old Cairo. We ate *ta'miyya* with pickles, strolled down the jewelry street, and priced gold bangles, as my grandfather used to do when it came close to my birthday. That night, on a hunch, I asked the concierge if there was a restaurant called Aboushakra. "It is a chain," he answered, "but the original one is not far from the hotel." We walked to the restaurant, sidestepping taxis and cars, their horns blaring incessantly under the hundreds of neon signs advertising Japanese electronic gadgets. Aboushakra had not changed in fifty years. Well, not completely. What had changed was the lighting and the advertising on the wall. As we entered the restaurant, I saw an enormous charcoal oven filled with tiny squab cooking. The room was uglier than I remembered, with dirty pink walls, fluorescent lights, and plastic baskets filled with toasted pita on each table. We ordered squab, *tehina*, vine leaves, hummus, and tomato salad with pickles. The tasty squab were sprinkled with cumin, garlic, and lime. We ate them with our fingers and laughed when we looked at our plates. Virtually no bones were left; we had chewed on everything.

The next day I called a journalist friend who had lived in Cairo for the last twenty years. Did she know where Sharia

Ismail Pasha was? She did not, but she had a friend who was mapping the old city for the government. The next day I drove to Salim Imbrahim's office. Salim, a tall man whose mustache curled upward at the ends like my grandfather's, greeted me warmly, pleased that I was interested in old Cairo. "When you were young," he explained, "Cairo was beautiful and Garden City had magnificent villas. Now half of them have been razed and replaced with ugly tall buildings. The forties were the glory days of Cairo." He paused, then asked with a sad smile, "Have you been to the Pyramids yet? A fence surrounds them now, and you must pay an entrance fee. Imagine that . . . an entrance fee! The Pyramids belong to Egyptians!" Salim brought out some old maps of Cairo. "This is the street," he said, pointing to a winding street starting at the Nile, "and here is number 22, your house. Let me take you there."

Juliette and I followed him eagerly to his car. Using the map, Salim easily found the street. The house was still there with its black gate, but the brass *P*'s were missing, and the veranda was now enclosed. The first floor housed an Egyptian retail bank. As we entered the courtyard, we were greeted by a guard dressed in European clothes. Salim explained who I was and wondered if the new owner of the house was there. The guard went in to see if I would be welcomed. A few minutes later we were ushered in. The staircase was as elegant as I remembered, but the large painting of my great-great grandmother was missing. I wondered where it was. As we entered the second-floor apartment, I stopped, astonished. Here were the same furnishings, arranged as they were when my grandparents lived there—but on the wrong floor. As I was whispering to my daughter about how these things had been in my youth, the owner, a man of at least eighty and wrapped in a silk dressing gown, approached us. "I am pleased to meet you," he said in perfect English; "I knew your grandparents well. I bought this house and all its belongings for a song. Come and see the living room." And there we sat on a white gilded couch, sipping thick Arab coffee, surrounded by petit point armchairs, listening to the old man telling us what a bargain this house had been. It was the very same white sofa I sat in for the old, yellowing picture taken when I was five. I looked around and felt a twinge of bitterness that nothing of my past belonged to me. I longed for the sofa. "Would you like to see the rest of the house?" he asked. I was eager to see the kitchen. It seemed smaller than I remembered and lacked the wonderful smells of Ahmet's cooking. I asked to see the back bedrooms. We were taken down a long corridor, where Renée and I used to play, into a small room overlooking the back garden. As we stepped onto the balcony, I saw the mango tree with ripe fruit hanging from its branches. I stood there for a minute recalling my grandfather's words of years ago. "When you were born, I planted a mango tree for my little princess."

The next day I followed Salim through the old part of Cairo to the market where years ago Ahmet and Grandmaman used to shop. Here, little had changed. The street was as noisy and as busy as it was years ago. The watermelon vendor was there with watermelons piled high. When I approached his stand, he grabbed a watermelon, took a knife, and cut out a chunk that he handed to me on his big knife. I bought the watermelon, as well as limes, small bananas, cherimoyas, and mangoes. We passed the bird man surrounded with cages filled with tiny squab and scrawny chickens. I could not recall a time when I was as happy as going through that market.

When we left, I thanked Salim and handed him my purchases, saying, "I live in a hotel. Please help yourself."

We took a taxi to the Zamaleck Sporting Club. We entered the swimming pool area, which was exactly as I had remembered it except that there were no women lounging about in their bathing suits. I learned that women were allowed in the swimming pool only on Thursdays, when the men were banned from sitting around playing cards or sipping drinks. The club still served tomato or cucumber sandwiches, which Juliette found to be tasteless. "How could you have liked these so much?" she asked. I had no answer for her.

That night we were invited to dinner by a journalist who lived in Meadi. The Meadi district, once a country retreat for well-to-do Europeans, was now totally built up to become a middle-class neighborhood with small villas and lots of elegant restaurants. While we munched on pepitas and pistachios on the journalist's terrace, I talked about my childhood and the changes I had noticed since I moved away. "Although more women cover their heads nowadays," he said, "many more women than ever hold important jobs and go to university here and abroad. We are striving to modernize, but we have problems. Too many people are leaving the countryside for Cairo. Cairo is bursting at the seams, and unemployment is high." His children were all university graduates and had the same concerns as Juliette. I recalled that I had little in common with my new French friends forty years ago. These young people were aware of what was happening in the world, liked the same music, read the same books and had the same dreams.

Over the next few days, we visited Groppi's once more; it looked seedier then ever, with only traces of its old splendor. We had small *ful* sandwiches in the street and, like tourists, visited all the important sites, stopping at the Mosque of Ibn Tallun, which my husband insisted that Juliette should not miss. We went back to the Khan-al-Khalili, bought slippers and fresh *loofas* to bring back home, coffee cups and silver jars filled with black kohl, and wooden sticks to apply it to my eyelids as I remembered my grandmother doing. Finally, Salim's map in hand, we went looking for the Convent of the Sacred Heart. As I hugged Mère de Rousiers in front of the statue of Our Lady of Lourdes, I thought of the small, lonely, and frightened girl entering the convent for the first time. I had lost a mother then, but at least I had had Cairo, a city and a family that nurtured me and that gave me a strong identity. I saw myself back in my dying mother's hospital room, trying in vain to sever the tie between the little girl and her mother. I looked once more at Our Lady of Lourdes, said a final goodbye to the orphan girl of Cairo. I was now ready to tell my story.